A TIPPERARY ESTATE:
Castle Otway, Templederry 1750–1853

Maynooth Studies in Local History

GENERAL EDITOR Raymond Gillespie

This is one of six new pamphlets published in 1998 in the Maynooth
Studies in Local History series. Like their fourteen predecessors these
volumes illustrate, through case studies of particular areas and themes, how life
in Ireland in the past evolved in a variety of settings, both urban and rural. As
such they join a rapidly growing literature dealing with the local dimension
of Ireland's past. That 'localness' is not primarily territorial, although all are
firmly rooted in a sense of place, but derives from an awareness of the regional
diversity of Irish society in the past.

Local history is not about administrative frameworks or geographical entities
but rather about the people who created the social worlds which made particular places distinctive. These pamphlets are therefore primarily about people
who lived in particular places over time. The range of people explored is wide;
from the poor of pre-famine Drogheda and Ferbane through the nouveau
riche world of the Meath grazier to the aristocratic lifestyle of an eighteenth-
century Tipperary landlord. What all these people have in common is that
they shaped their particular places in response to stimuli both from within
their communities and from the wider world.

Like their predecessors these pamphlets allow us a brief glimpse into the
diverse, interacting worlds which are the basis of the Irish historical experience.
In their own right they are each significant contributions to our understanding of that experience in all its richness and complexity. They present
local history as the vibrant and challenging discipline that it is.

Maynooth Studies in Local History: Number 17

A Tipperary Estate:
Castle Otway, Templederry 1750–1853

Miriam Lambe

IRISH ACADEMIC PRESS

First published in 1998 by
IRISH ACADEMIC PRESS
44, Northumberland Road, Dublin 4, Ireland
and in North America by
IRISH ACADEMIC PRESS
c/o ISBS, 5804 NE Hassalo Street, Portland, OR 97213
website: http://www.iap.ie

© Miriam Lambe 1998

British Library Cataloguing in Publication Data

Lambe, Miriam
   A Tipperary landed estate: Castle Otway 1750–1853.
   (Maynooth studies in local history) 1. Otway (Family)
   2. Landlord and tenant – Ireland – Tipperary – History –
   18th century 3. Landlord and tenant – Ireland – Tipperary
   – History – 19th century – 4. Tipperary (Ireland) – Social
   conditions – History 5. Tippeary (Ireland) – Social life and
   customs – History 6. Tipperary (Ireland) – Economic
   conditions – History
   I. Title
   333.5'4'094192'09033

   ISBN 0–7165–2705–7

Typeset in 10 pt on 12 pt Bembo by
Carrigboy Typesetting Services, County Cork
Printed by ColourBooks Ltd., Dublin

Contents

Preface

In the course of researching and writing this pamphlet many people have helped me by providing energy, knowledge and support. I would particularly like to thank those who contributed substantially to the overall structure and focus of the pamphlet, Bernadette Cunningham, Dr Raymond Gillespie and Dr Mary Ann Lyons. The feedback from Dr Jacqueline Hill, supervisor for my Master of Arts thesis, who suggested ways of improving drafts of the thesis was appreciated.

For the financial assistance given by the Marino Institute of Education, I would like to thank Dr Dónal Leader, cfc. My colleague Br Rory Geoghegan, cfc, introduced me to the world of spreadsheets.

The greatest debt I owe is to my supportive family and in particular to my husband Eddie Fogarty who gave me not only time and space in which to create my thesis but also acted as unofficial editor and proof reader.

Introduction

The Otway estate, the origins of which will be discussed at a later stage, lies close to the village of Templederry, roughly nine miles south east of Nenagh, and six miles north west of the town of Borrisoleigh, in the foothills of the Devil's Bit-Slieve Felim mountains (see figure 1). An advertisement in 1778 for the letting of land in Kilnafinch, close to the Otway estate, emphasised the advantageous location of the property, close to the 'good market town' of Silvermines and 'within two miles of the great fair of Toomevara'.[1] The estate was composed of two separate units, Lissenhall which was outside Nenagh, on the road to Newport, and Castle Otway, the subject of this pamphlet. Lack of information makes it difficult to calculate accurately the size of the estate in terms of its acreage in the early part of the period under review. However, it is known that in 1852 the Castle Otway estate consisted of 6,667 statute acres.[2] A document compiled in 1775, by Henry Prittie, of Kilboy, Dolla, a neighbour and relation of Thomas Otway, is a useful indication of the income generated from this estate. He compiled a list of the principal landholders in County Tipperary, numbering 129 landowners, together with an estimate of their annual income, which ranged from £14,000 to £400 per annum. The income of the Otway estate was put at £2,000. Prittie himself had an income of £8,000.[3]

The following extract from the Primary School Folklore Collection, while it is specific to one individual landlord, neatly encapsulates the deeply entrenched image of the landlord in Irish folklore and literature.

> The landlord of Clonsast, Rathgangan, County Kildare was Lord Ashtown. If a person got a new coat he would raise the rent ... No man was allowed to sow the second crop with [sic] manuring the ground or if he did he would be evicted. He built a protestant school in Brackna, Clonsast, and said that he would make the Catholic people go to that school and let their school go to waste. No person was allowed to sell a load of turf or if he was caught he would be put out of his house. He put protestants into houses and the Catholics were put out and they had to go to the poor house or die by the roadside ...

This pamphlet will examine the relationship between a particular family of landlords and those who lived on the property and will consider the stereotype that prevails. While the perception of the landlord-tenant relationship has

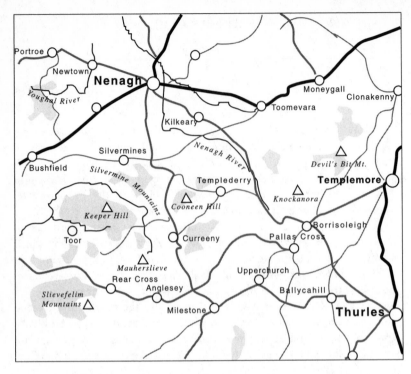

1. Location map of Castle Otway Templederry, Co. Tipperary.

been challenged by academic historians, at a local level it is still deeply
ingrained.[4]

Historical research is about asking questions and some of the questions
which will be asked in the course of this investigation are: how big was the
Otway estate community? how and when did its size fluctuate? how did it
earn its living? how far were the people bound together? on what issues were
they divided? what were its links with the wider world?

The period selected for this essay, 1750–1853, was partly predetermined by
the extant primary source material; the estate papers. Separate from this con-
sideration was the fact that this period was significant both in terms of national
events and of the history of the estate. In the context of national history
1750–1850 was a time of considerable economic development in Ireland.
Agricultural output soared, for example, benefiting from increased demand for
Irish produce arising, in one particular period, from the Napoleonic wars.[5]
Hand in hand with the growth in the economy went a demographic explosion.
The period 1750–1850 can be described as one demographic cycle, beginning
with the recovery in terms of population from the famine of 1740–1 and
ending with the Great Famine of 1845. Although the accuracy of the early

nineteenth-century census returns have been questioned, nonetheless the figures confirm the population increase. At the local level of the parish the experience of Templederry was in line with the rest of the country: the population grew between 1821 and 1841 and declined from then onwards.

Table 1. Population of Templederry 1821–1851				
Parish	1821	1831	1841	1851
Latteragh	968	995	1131	745
Templederry	1764	1857	2032	1457

Source: *Census Ire.*, 1821, 1831, 1841, 1851.

The ramifications of this demographic growth, in terms of its effects on scarce resources, are important in a local history study. At the estate level there were important changes on the local landscape, namely the construction of the residence, Castle Otway, in the middle decades of the eighteenth-century. By the close of the period the estate suffered a reversal in its fortunes and by 1853 the bankrupt estate was advertised for auction by the landed estates courts.[6]

In the case of the Otway papers, the collection is a small one and is not chronologically complete, with the result that some periods will be covered in more depth than others. Arising from these gaps in the primary documentation this reconstruction of the community will be more in the nature of a series of snapshots of the community, at intervals in its past. To supplement this material and to put the Otway estate community into a wider context this study has drawn on other sources of information, particularly on parliamentary papers and the working papers of government departments. The middle decades of the nineteenth-century saw an increase in the number of provincial newspapers published in Ireland. It was not until the division of Tipperary into two ridings in 1838 and the emergence of Nenagh as the county town of the north riding that a newspaper was established in that town. The two most important newspapers covering the Nenagh area and by extension the Templederry area were the *Nenagh Guardian* and the *Tipperary Vindicator*. The *Guardian* was first published in July 1838 and the latter newspaper in January 1844. Like some newspapers of to-day, the provincial press of the nineteenth-century reflected the views of their proprietors and editors. Maurice Lenihan, editor of the *Tipperary Vindicator* referred to the *Nenagh Guardian*, as indeed did Daniel O'Connell, as 'my contemporary, the orange rag'.[7] The following item in the *Tipperary Vindicator* was reprinted from the *Times* in March 1844

The *Tipperary Vindicator* is a journal which started on Repeal and ultra radical principles and therefore any general charges it may think proper to prefer against either landlords or their agents must be received with caution.[8]

Tipperary has been the subject of study by several scholars, both geographers and historians.[9] The geographers have tended to emphasise the importance of the landscape and in the case of W.J. Smyth, of the role of the landlord in shaping that landscape.[10] Historians of County Tipperary tend to have a politics-centred view of the county and for much of the period under review local politics would have been very much the preserve of county society. Thomas Power's study of eighteenth-century Tipperary and the more recent book entitled *The two Tipperarys* while being excellent studies of what has been called 'county society' and the networking of the landed class, add little to what is known about those who were on the fringes of society, those who were disenfranchised, either by virtue of class or religion or both.[11]

The contribution this pamphlet makes is to spotlight an area of north Tipperary described by William Head, a land owner, as a 'district dotted over with small landowners', which, from an archival point of view, results in a lack of readily available estate papers relating to this area.[12] This investigation restores the balance of the historiography of County Tipperary, which heretofore has concentrated on the larger estates. While the central theme is that of the landlord-tenant relationship the inquiry proposes to recreate, in so far as it is possible from the evidence available, an image of the historical reality of the Otway estate community. This community was distinguished from other groups of people in the area by the religious and ethnic composition of its members and above all, by the ties of having the same landlord: the Otway family.

The first chapter will focus primarily on the period from 1750 to the beginning of the nineteenth-century with the emphasis on Thomas Otway as landlord. The estate records which have survived for the eighteenth-century were created during his tenure as landlord. The estate in the nineteenth-century will be covered in the second chapter with a change of focus from landlord to tenants. In the third chapter the evidence will be used to investigate the internal interactions of the Castle Otway community, or group dynamics.

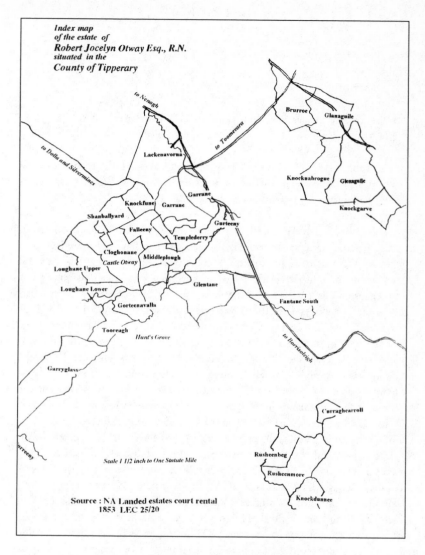

Index map
of the estate of
Robert Jocelyn Otway Esq., R.N.
situated in the
County of Tipperary

to Nenagh

to Toomevara

Brurroe

Glanaguile

to Dolla and Silvermines

Lackenavorna

Knocknabrogue

Glenaguile

Knockfune

Garrane

Garrane

Knockgarve

Shanballyard

Gurteeny

Falleeny

Templederry

Cloghonane
Castle Otway

Middleplough

Loughane Upper

Loughane Lower

Glentane

Gorteenavalla

Fantane South

Tooreagh

Hunt's Grove

to Borrisoleigh

Garryglass

Curraghcarroll

arreeny

Scale 1 1/2 inch to One Statute Mile

Rusheenbeg

Rusheenmore

Knockdunnee

Source : NA Landed estates court rental
1853 LEC 25/20

2. Map of the Otway Estate 1852

The Landlord

The Otway family was descended from a Westmoreland soldier, John Otway who

> espouse [sic] the cause of Cromwell and following the fortunes of the usurper into Ireland acquired by his sword a considerable property in that county . . . known as Castle Otway.[1]

The Cromwellian land settlement altered the structure of landownership in this part of Tipperary, as in many other areas, by changing the ethnic and religious structure of its population. The commissioners conducting the Civil Survey which was held to establish land-ownership prior to its redistribution met in Nenagh in July 1654. The Civil Survey shows, that before the Cromwellian settlement, unlike the southern part of County Tipperary, land in Upper Ormond, in which Castle Otway is situated, was found to be have been traditionally held in fractions, by kinship groups of native origin.[2] The principal names of the barony of Upper Ormond were listed as 'Hogane, Kennedy, Glysane, and Ryan.'[3] 'Daniell Kennedy of Ballintotta, Dermod Kenedy of Shanballyard and Richard Butler of Kylcash, all Irish papists' were returned as owning two ploughlands in 'Fallyny and Cloghonane'.[4]

Lands which were forfeited in north Tipperary were reserved for division among the army. Lieutenant John Otway, the first Otway to be associated with this area, was confirmed in the ownership of his lands by Charles II with the exception of those lands in Latteragh which were restored to the Morris family.[5] Otway added to his original land grant by purchasing from soldiers debentures for land. In August 1660 he purchased seventy-three acres in Latteragh from John Stafford of Sligo which the latter had received for 'arrears of £46.11s.7d. for service in Ireland'. The purchase price was £15.[6] The period which followed the Cromwellian transfer of ownership of land saw the establishment of single ownership of estates and while more native Irish went to Connaught from Tipperary than from any other county, many remained in the area as tenants of the new English Protestant landlords.[7]

A second and lasting effect of the seventeenth-century change in land-ownership was the alteration in the ethnic and religious structure of the area. The poll money return of 1659, a couple of years after the Cromwellian land settlement, gives the population of 'Lafferagh' as fifty-nine Irish and in the townland of Cloghonan, in which Castle Otway is situated, there were four Irish. No English were returned despite a 'John O Howay Esq.' being listed as the principal landowner there.[8] Latteragh is the civil parish which adjoins, and now forms part of, the Roman Catholic parish of Templederry. The Protestant population in north Tipperary was predominantly of English descent and it would appear that the forfeited lands were settled by people from the planted counties of Laois and Offaly rather than by further immigration from England.[9]

In the mid-eighteenth century several landlords attempted to attract Protestant tenants to Upper Ormond. The *Clonmel Gazette* advertised the letting of the lands of Cooneen and also some houses in the town of Silvermines by Henry Prittie with the stipulation that 'good encouragement will be given to Protestant families who would covenant to reside'.[10] William Barker of Kilcooley sponsored the settlement of Palatines on his estate and some of the names of tenants found on the Otway estate, Baskerville and Shouldice, suggest that Thomas Otway may have also encouraged such migration.[11] The Protestant element of the community grew in the early years of the nineteenth century, according to the minister at Templederry, who reported that the fifty Protestant families in the parish represented an increase 'in consequence of encouragement from the landlords to settle here.'[12] The name Powell first appears in the Otway records in 1825 when a Caleb Powell was listed as renting the Coppice apparently having moved to Templederry from Moneygall.[13] That diversity of composition of the community was characteristic of this part of Upper Ormond is apparent from the commission of inquiry into Irish education in 1826. According to this report there were twenty-nine Protestants attending school in Templederry and twenty-two in the neighbouring townland of Kilboy. In the adjoining parishes of Borrisoleigh and Upperchurch, both in the barony of Kilnamanagh, no Protestant children were returned as attending school.[14] The Protestant population of the combined civil parishes of Latteragh and Templederry was given as 155, of whom 118 lived in Templederry, out of a total population of 2,987 people.[15] Thus for some of the tenantry on the Otway estate there were ties other than that of landlord and tenant, the landlord and these tenants were part of the same spiritual community.

Between the years 1731 and 1853 Castle Otway had a number of owners (see Appendix 1). The line of succession was complicated as several of the owners died without heirs and were succeeded by brothers or, in the case of Robert Otway Cave, MP, (d.1844), first by his wife Sophie and then by a cousin Robert Jocelyn Otway.[16] Down to 1800 the Otways were resident landlords. Henry Otway married Sarah Cave in 1799 and they resided on her Northamptonshire estates, Stanford Hall in Leicester or in Grosvenor Square, London. All of their children were baptised in Northamptonshire and Henry Otway was buried in the same county.[17] From the time of Henry's inheriting Castle Otway from his father Cook Otway (d. 1800), the Otway family became absentee landlords.[18]

1750 the Otway family was very much established as part of the Tipperary gentry. Their sons and daughters married within the gentry class, the family was related by marriage to Lord Norbury, to the Cardens of Templemore, to Lord Bloomfield of Ciamaltha House, near Newport, County Tipperary. Thomas Otway married Martha Prittie of Kilboy in 1757, his brother, Cooke, who later succeeded him in the estate married Elizabeth Waller of Newport and their daughter, also named Martha, married Francis Aldborough Prittie. The life stories of the sons of Castle Otway followed the predictable paths of sons of the gentry. The aforesaid Thomas Otway was educated at Trinity College, Dublin. His nephews Henry and Samuel were also educated at Trinity College, Dublin and Samuel continued his education at Oxford and eventually took holy orders. Robert Waller Otway was an admiral in the royal navy and two other nephews pursued careers in the army. The landed gentry had obligations in local government and in the administration of justice, and members of the Otway family fulfilled its duties by serving as justices of the peace and as members of the grand jury.

The building of Cloghonan Castle, later known as Castle Otway, in the middle of the eighteenth century, was important not only in that the physical landscape was altered but also as indicating a transition in the mind set of the family.[19] In the townland of Cloghonan the Civil Survey noted the existence of a 'castle partly repaired'.[20] The new house, 'into which part of an old castle enters' can be seen as a manifestation that the siege mentality had been eradicated from the mental landscape of the Otway family, the residence was now an oasis of gentility, respectability and refinement.[21] Castle Otway which was designed on classical lines, stood as a symbol of the position and aspirations of the Otway family now secure in their physical environment and settled socially and with their role in the local and wider county community and indeed of the metropolitan society of London.

Thomas Otway who died in 1786, has been portrayed as a harsh and stern landlord on the basis of entries in his estate ledgers. For example, one entry noted that a spalpeen ran away even though he had money due to him.[22] There is no doubt that Thomas Otway used the threat of eviction and of fines as a means of managing his property. His steward, Alex Caldwell, issued several notices in 1771 on behalf of his employer. One gave notice that the tenants and workmen who did not come to work on 'any holyday (except Sunday)' would be fined a 'shilling each for the first time, any person living on his land not satisfied with this law may provide for himself another place'.[23] The same ledger records the imposition of financial penalties for various transgressions of the estate rules. Fines were imposed for not unyoking cars or carts properly. After a fifth offence, in the case of a cottier the house was to be pulled down. If the offender were a spalpeen 'he is never to work a day at Castle Otway more'. In June 1772 Silo Magher was fined for speaking Irish before the master. Philip Doughney, John Ryan, Timothy, Michael and Patrick Kennedy were

3. Castle Otway, Templederry, 1997 (from a photograph
taken by Eddie Fogarty)

penalised because the master's harrow was 'stole by some of Loughane men'.
In this case the fine was 1*d*. However, this fine was subsequently cancelled.

To simply highlight the fines imposed by the landlord ignores the complexity of the relationship between landlord and tenant. There were often
extenuating circumstances for imposing fines. Bramlet Wright was ordered not
to work at Castle Otway for a year 'for admitting the children Henry and Loftus
to the car and leaving them to the mercy of the horse and providence'.[24] John
Dun was disciplined for a similar offence.

In April 1779 cottiers were again warned that those who absented themselves
from work 'except Sundays and Christmas' would be charged '30*s*. a collop for
their cattle and 30*s*. an acre for garden'.[25] A simplistic interpretation would be to
see this threat as being motivated by sectarianism with the Protestant landlord
preventing the Catholic cottiers fulfilling their religious obligations. But the
practice of observing the requirement to attend Mass on Sundays and holy days
and abstain from servile work was not firmly established in Ireland prior to the
Famine. Indeed such were the social problems associated with holy days and
pattern days that the Catholic hierarchy abrogated two feast days in 1829,
Easter Monday and the feast of St. John the Baptist. They failed in 1831 to
reach agreement on the abrogation of most of the remaining ten holy days.[26]

This 'arbitrary system of punishment' may have been motivated by a
concern with anti-social behaviour, and in particular with that resulting from

alcohol abuse. [27] One spalpeen was fined for absenting himself from work to attend the fair. A report filed by the Castle Otway constabulary in 1838 may clarify why Thomas Otway would have wished to discourage unnecessary attendance at a fair day. On this particular day in 1838 while there were only fifty head of cattle on sale there were thirty-eight tents selling liquor. The day passed quietly until the tents were struck and later that evening fourteen people were arrested for drunkenness and causing a riot. [28]

Other fines seem to have been motivated by a desire to effect change and improvement in work practices. Labour shortages gave workers a definite advantage in establishing the actual day to day substance of a working relationship between master and servant, one aspect of which might have been a certain degree of tolerance of worker misbehaviour or absenteeism. That the landlord was in a position to impose penalties for unacceptable work practices may be more revealing of a shift in the balance of power to the landlord consequent on a growth in population. Several workmen were each fined 1s.1d.

> to spoiling the sea cole beds, not doing as ordered by the master viz. to weed the beds first perfectly clean and then to cover 'em with one inch of sand only, whereas you covered 'em without weeding 4 inches deep with sand. Ordered by the master that they take off all the sand again, and that you get no pay until the beds are properly cleaned and finished. [29]

Another worker was fined for 'neglecting to have the stones picked off the fallow field 'tho often ordered'.

The Dublin Society, in April 1767, presented Thomas Otway with a silver medal 'in testimony of the Society's approbation of his laudable spirit for the improvement of his county'. [30] The improvements which he had carried out involved draining, ditching and planting. Having been proposed and seconded at the same meeting he was elected a member of the Society. The estate ledgers record payments made by workers for tools supplied and this was probably an effort by Otway to introduce different farm implements to the estate. A shovel cost from 1s. to 1s.7d., a scythe and stone 3s.3d., a reaping hook 1s.1d. [31] Some of the tools were brought in from outside; a saw was purchased in Dublin for 6s.6d. and a handsaw from Limerick cost 3s. One tenant bought a saddle costing 6s.5½d. from the landlord. This practice of buying farm implements from outside continued in the next century when Thomas Ryan, the steward, was reimbursed his expenses in bringing farm implements from Holyhead to Dublin, to Castle Otway. [32] To what extent estate practice influenced the farming methods of tenants and cottiers, it is difficult to say. There is, however, a record of the estate supplying seed to tenants in 1845. Turnip seed was sold to twenty-seven tenants including Abraham Harrington who got 3lb of seed at 1s.6d. per pound while Martin Kenny was sold 2oz of parsnip seed. [33]

Again reflecting his association with the Dublin Society, Thomas Otway promoted the production of textiles on his estate, both linen and wool. The extent of the industry, however, is unclear. There are records of seed being supplied by the landlord and of goods being supplied to the castle. Bamlet Wright of Middleplough grew flax as did Mick Ryan Counsellor, the seed seemingly being provided by the estate. Judy Darmody sold flax seed in Nenagh.[34] In 1779 Charles MacDaniel was paid for 34 yards of linen for a table cloth, the following year he supplied 24½ yards of grey linen at 2s. a yard. Joe Wright and his wife were allowed against their rent for supplying 50lbs of carpet wool. Molly Wright was supplied with 6 lbs. of wool to spin 'candleweek'.

The degree to which the landlord encouraged the settlement of weavers in the area is uncertain as only one deed has survived, that of a lease made between Thomas Otway and Charles MacDaniel, linen weaver, of one acre and one rood of garden in Templederry at an annual rent of £4.11s.0d. for three lives. This lease was dated 1773.[35] There are many questions concerning the production of textiles on the Otway which must remain unanswered. How many tenants were involved in spinning or weaving either linen or wool? Were there others as well as the McDaniels and the Wrights? How extensive was the growing of flax? One field in Falleeny is still known to the owner as the 'flax field'.[36] How long did the production of linen survive in the area? The MacDaniel family is recorded in the rent rolls as late as 1806, the original lease of 1773 being relinquished in April 1810 but whether they were still involved in linen production is unknown.[37] Some of these questions may be answered by referring in general terms to the linen industry which failed generally in the south of Ireland. The trade was moderately active in 1770 and 1771 but it never recovered after the depression of 1773. A parliamentary report of 1763 stated that there were no linen markets established in Tipperary and what activity there was centred on flax growing. By 1816 linen in County Tipperary was primarily manufactured for home user.[38] The surveyor of the Primary Valuation in 1845 noted that a mill at Garrane had 'two willows for breaking wool and two carding machines . . . which worked for five months of the year, ten hours a day'.[39]

Some of the estate improvements would have been of greater benefit to the landlord than the tenants, for example the investment in a deer park and also in the plantations, beech and scotch pines were among the varieties planted. However, there were spin offs from these developments in the form of additional employment opportunities. There are references to tenants and labourers being paid for drawing sand and turf to the castle, others provided house wattles and rushes, repaired walls. Indeed some employment was given to people from outside the estate, from the townlands of Ballydaff in Glenkeen, Gortnalara and Rathanure, Templederry, noteably Mick Brien, Ballincara, also in Templederry, who was paid for drawing sand and turf.[40]

That the transition from one owner to another could be difficult was high-lighted by the *Tipperary Vindicator* in December 1844 when it reported that Lord Hawarden 'of exterminating notoriety' was lord in waiting to the queen and Admiral Robert Otway 'inheritor of the princely estates of the ever-to-be lamented Mr. Otway Cave' was groom in waiting to the queen. The editor expressed the hope 'that the latter will not allow himself to imbibe the heartless principles of the former'.[41] The repercussions of a change in ownership was underscored by a report compiled by the Catholic curate of Templederry in 1880 on rackrents.[42] Lord Dunalley's first exercise of his ownership, Fr Glynn said was to 'serve middleman and tenants with writs of ejectment, next to raise the rents'. As this report was compiled during the Land War the bias of Fr Glynn's observations must be acknowledged.

Very little is known about Thomas Otway's brother and heir, Cooke Otway, as few of the estate records which have survived relate to the period of his ownership. A letter, written by Cooke Otway to his law agent in November 1789, would indicate that the estate was already in financial difficulties at the end of the eighteenth century. Otway was querying the delay in 'Harry's marriage settlement being fixed', he was fearful that the match would be lost if the matter was not sorted.[43] The match was worth £3,000 English at a time when there were assignments of £2,000 Irish judgments against the estate. The absence of estate rentals for this period makes it difficult to establish the cause or causes of this indebtedness, whether it was overspending on conspicuous consumption or the inability of the estate to adjust to changing economic circumstances. Such was the extent of these difficulties that the family initiated a private act of parliament to try and solve their financial problems.[44] They did not, however, proceed with the matter. Cooke Otway is reputed to have acted in a harsh manner during the 1798 rebellion and in 1800 Mathew Gleeson and James Flannery were transported for seven years for their part in a 'fruitless conspiracy to punish Otway for his actions during the suppression of the 1798 rebellion'.[45] It has not as yet been possible to substantiate these claims.

Robert Otway Cave who inherited from his father Henry in 1815 was MP first for Leicester, 1826–30, and then for Tipperary from 1832 until his death in 1844. In entering politics Otway Cave was following a family tradition, albeit of his mother's ancestors, Caves having served as MPs for Leicester city between 1710 and 1790. His election to parliament for Leicester in 1826 was shrouded in controversy as he had been selected by the corporation of Leicester on the understanding that he would not support Catholic emancipation. There was a disagreement over the expenses of the election between Otway Cave and the corporation with the result that Otway Cave became assiduous in

> bringing all its misdemeanours to the notice of parliament. His malevolence was noted without approval by his leader Peel. Cave even turned his coat over Catholic emancipation, presenting a petition from Leicester in favour of the measure and in the end voting for it.[46]

In a letter published in 1844 in the *Tipperary Vindicator* Otway Cave expressed his delight at the election of Nicholas Maher, who was a Catholic, as MP, at the expense of the 'Tory-Orange' faction.[47] Otway Cave, in his support for Catholic emancipation and the abolition of tithes, would have found common ground among a significant section of his tenantry. On his death in 1844, Maurice Lenihan, who could never be described as impartial, eulogised Otway Cave in the following words 'when we speak in high terms of his conduct as a landlord we but reecho the sentiments cherished towards him by a numerous respectable and affluent tenantry'.[48]

During the first half of the nineteenth century the Otways were absentee landlords, nevertheless their visits to their Irish estates were sufficiently long to allow participation in local affairs. The *Tipperary Vindicator* announced that during his sojourn at the castle, Mr. Otway Cave would attend the forthcoming assizes as one of the grand jurors. The contact with their Irish estates was reinforced by correspondence with various agents and employees. They were thus well informed on estate matters and had a more than passing acquaintance with their tenantry. Writing from Bristol in November 1848 to her solicitor, William Stephens, Mrs. Otway Cave informed him that 'young Waddick has written to me requesting me to send him and his mother and sister to America'.[49] She later requested her agent to do what Waddick wanted and 'give him £25, his wife's father to contribute what more may be necessary'.[50]

In discussions with her agent and solicitor concerning designs for a proposed new priest's house, Mrs. Otway Cave, who was not a Catholic, said that it was 'very desirable to have a priest resident amongst the people of Templederry . . . of course he must have a fitting habitation'.[51] From a letter which Fr John Kenyon, the Young Ireland priest, wrote to Mrs. Otway Cave, it would appear that the relationship between the chapel and the castle was sufficiently cordial to the extent that Fr Kenyon and his 'zealous French friends' were entertained at the castle by Mrs. Otway Cave.[52]

In her correspondence Mrs. Otway Cave also expressed her concern at the plight of the people of Templederry during the famine of 1845. 'It would not', she said

> be amiss to suggest to him [Fr Kenyon] urging on his flock a few simple precautions for their own sake against the fearfully prevailing disease, explaining to them the vital importance of them, for unless one can make the people sensible of this, any measures one may take are almost useless.[53]

She was 'happy to do anything you think likely to be of use to them as we are threatened in addition to all other evils with a visitation of cholera'. As a precaution, dung heaps and pools of water at cabin doors were to be cleared, 'the sooner the better some labourers are set to work in that way the better'.[54] In January 1848 she ordered that that the 'planting on Stapleton's hill and on

Knockadigeen be started in the spring', because there was 'no use in not giving work any longer'.

It was Mrs. Otway Cave's view that free trade had a great effect on the letting of land, she wondered how 'it would have been possible to have kept the people from starving if the repeal of the corn laws had not preceded the famine'. It would be, she said 'a great blessing if the blight returned to show the insanity of trusting to the potato'. She continued in her letter that

> the great danger to guard against is the people falling back again upon them as their ordinary food . . . do what you must to prevent it and thus frustrating all the hopes of those beneficial results which were the only consolation for the terrible suffering of those last two years.[55]

A return to the old ways was, she feared inevitable as some landlords for selfish motives 'instead of checking rather encourage a return to the old system'.

In the management of an estate in the eighteenth and nineteenth centuries the agent and steward were important links between the landlord and tenants. The activities, disposition and character of these estate personnel were all important in determining how the landlord and tenants interacted with each other and their perceptions of each other. It was also in the agent's own interest to keep tenants' indebtedness to a minimum as the agent was paid a commission of about 20 per cent on rents collected.[56] The roles of agent and steward were of even greater significance in the case of an absentee landlord. A Mr. Wilson was considered suitable, by Rev. S.J. Otway, as agent, and he was of the opinion that there should not be

> animosity to him on account of the tenants it was found advisable to remove from this part of your property [Lissenhall] and I expect he will not meet with any annoyances as your tenantry have their farms at moderate rents and ought to be satisfied.[57]

Mrs. Otway Cave, writing to her solicitor in November 1848 stressed the necessity of having 'a proper responsible head-man with a position and authority adequate to his situation under whatever name is resident at Castle Otway. I see this necessity the clearer the more I reflect upon all that has occurred since I left it'.[58]

From the records it can be established who some of these key personnel were. Alex Caldwell was agent under Thomas Otway and he resided in Nelson Hall, Templederry. He was succeeded by Charles Simons, of whom nothing is known. A Thomas Ryan was steward in the early years of the nineteenth century. The fact that Thomas Ryan was also a tenant might have made him more circumspect in his dealings with the tenants who were after all his own neighbours. He could sympathise with them because in 1816 his own rent was in arrears of £41.18s.1d.

In May 1827 Daniel Carr, steward, wrote to Robert Otway Cave, in London, giving an account of the difficulties he was experiencing with the tenants of Moanroan who were in arrears with their bog rents. A Mr. Geasham sent people to the bog 'in defiance of notice not to cut turf'. He asks if it were possible for Otway Cave to spend 'at least one week here . . . if your health permits . . . if not it will not be in my power to settle with or get out a great many of your Lissenhall tenants'.[59] There was a suggestion that the difficulties experienced by this particular individual may have been because he was English. Patrick Kennedy, MD, in a letter to the *Tipperary Vindicator*, in 1844, stated that the claim of evictions on the property of Otway Cave was a 'whole fabrication'.[60] He went on to explain that the evictions in question had taken place twenty years previously when an Englishman named Carr, who was the agent, found many of the tenants in arrears and their farms divided, 'Otway Cave did not retain him longer than eighteen months and since then there have been no evictions'.

Thomas Ryan was replaced as agent by Thomas Ryder Pepper who appears to have been appointed to the position sometime after the death of Henry Otway in 1815. Ryder Pepper was a member of the gentry, he resided at Laughton, near Moneygal, County Tipperary. He was a brother-in-law of Lord Bloomfield who, in turn, was related to Henry Otway Cave. As Robert Otway Cave was only nineteen at the time of his father's death it was probably felt that Pepper was a more prudent choice as agent. As a member of the gentry he would have a different approach to dealing with the tenants. It was perhaps this class difference which made him vulnerable to attack as it was reported that he was waylaid by two armed men in 1834, who demanded the money which he had collected in rents.[61]

During periods when the landlord and his key personnel shared a common background, there was no automatic guarantee that the landlord's interests would be protected. Cooke Otway wrote a letter, in 1788, to his law agent, Cooper Crawford, who was also from a local landed family, remarking that it would be interesting to see his agent suing himself on behalf of Otway. A dispute had arisen over a wall which Cooper had built blocking access from Castle Otway to Tiermoyle where Crawford had land. Otway said he preferred 'pen and ink to sledge and pick-ax' as a means of settling the dispute.[62]

The validity of previous assessments of the Otway family as landlords is questionable. The Otway family has been indiscriminately described as a 'family of stern landlords whose house was burned in 1920' and in particular Thomas Otway has been maligned as a 'stern landlord'.[63] This evaluation has been reached by relying primarily on the evidence from one source, the ledgers which have survived from the years 1771–2, 1778–80 and which relate to Thomas Otway's period as landlord. However these same ledgers contain counterbalancing evidence. The rate at which John Butler was charged for his potato ground was reduced from 7s. an acre to 6s. in recognition of 'you

having cleared so much in work'.[64] The fine imposed on the workers because
a harrow was stolen was subsequently cancelled. There are also references to
people being allowed sums of money for the 'customary Christmas dinner'.
During the early years of the nineteenth-century regular donations, of a charitable nature, were made by the landlord, for example, to Dean Holme's charity
school, to the dispensary in the Silvermines.[65] Other discretionary payments
are listed. In 1811 Mrs. Julian Bourke of Garryglass was in receipt of a yearly
allowance or present of £6.5s.3d. which was to 'cease on the 1 May 1814'.[66]
The accounts for January 1823 note 'presents to tenantry by yr [sic] written
order', the cost being £6.10s.0½d.[67]

The views of earlier researchers who wrote of the relations between the
Otway landlords and their tenants are seriously distorted because they failed
to discriminate between the different owners and thus allow for changes in
the mind sets and management styles of the individuals who owned the estate
at a particular time.

In the following chapter the focus of attention will be on the people who
lived within the estate boundaries, particularly in the early nineteenth-century.
The role of the landlord will be examined from the point of controlling access
to land and thus in influencing the socio-economic structure of the community.

The Tenantry

Much of what is known about Irish rural society between the famine of 1741 and that beginning in 1845 is derived from a variety of sources, the observations of travellers such as Mr. and Mrs. Hall and Arthur Young, the statistical surveys commissioned by the Dublin Society and sundry parliamentary inquiries into poverty and landholding.[1] The evidence derived from these sources is frequently of an impressionistic nature as they often lack specific data. However during the nineteenth-century more and more information of a statistical kind was collected by the government. Of particular value are the census data of population and agriculture.

Similar difficulties are encountered with the sources which are indigenous to the Otway estate, namely the account books, rent rolls and leases. Up to the period 1806, the evidence lends itself more to an impressionistic interpretation of the data while statistical analysis is possible on the information which survives for the later period, 1806 to 1850. The sources conveniently divide into two groups, those records which were produced while the Otway family was resident in Ireland and those which reflect the administration of the estate by absentee landlords. The estate material thus allows a comparison to be made of the structure of the community under a resident landlord and a non-resident landlord as well as before and after 1815.

Because of the way in which the information was recorded in the estate ledgers which cover the 1770s it is not practical to analyse the records quantitatively with a view to accurately reconstructing the economic and social structure of the estate at that time. Many of the entries fail to adequately identify or distinguish between people with the same name and it is difficult to differentiate between those who were resident on the estate and those who were not, as addresses were not routinely recorded. However the records do give a picture of the structure of the community, at the end of the 1770s, and the overwhelming impression is that of a complex community.

The socio-economic structure of the Otway estate could be described as a pyramid, broadly based at the bottom with cottiers and spalpeens, narrowing towards the top with the landlord at the apex. The tenant farmers formed the middle rank. This community was made up of cottiers, spalpeens, tenant farmers, artisans, artisan farmers, and their wives and children. The tenant farmers could be further divided into those who were freeholders and those who were not, and those who could be categorised as middlemen. While exact figures are not available, it would appear that cottiers were more numerous than any other economic or social sector. This disproportionate number of cottiers was probably owing to the fact that much of the estate was farmed directly by the landlord as distinct from being leased to tenant farmers. The evidence which suggests this interpretation comes from the extant leases.

A cottier would rent a house and garden and perhaps some potato ground, while wages due were offset against the rent. Grazing was allocated on the basis of 'collops', the rent for the grazing of a cow was generally 6s. A garden was available at 20s. an acre. Some cottiers also had access to meadow in Garryglass, Mick Butler had part of a meadow there at a rent of 8s., while Garret Burn paid £1.9s.0d. for half a meadow in the same townland.[2] There were additional charges which a cottier might have had to pay. Tools may have been purchased from the estate, the landlord might have paid hearth tax on a cottier's behalf.[3] Some cottiers' accounts included tithe charges.

The estate accounts are unequivocal in showing that, even within this small community, resources were unevenly distributed. Some examples will illustrate this reality. Tim Lee had three cows on two acres, seven perches of garden. In addition to the annual charge of £5.5s.0d. for his house and garden, Charles MacDaniel, the weaver, paid for the grass of four cows and one horse and he also had access to commonage. Paddy Collins and his sons grazed six sheep in Garryglass. Pat Cleary had three sheep and some pigs for which he purchased two stone of potatoes from the estate. Mick Ryan 'Counsellor' kept five cows and a horse.[4]

The estate was engaged in both arable and pastoral farming and the labour requirements of the estate were met by the cottiers and tenant farmers. They were employed for sowing, weeding planting, mowing, harvesting and threshing crops. A variety of crops were grown, 'sea cole', wheat, oats, turnips. Work was also available drawing sand and turf. Rates of pay varied from 3d. per day for threshing a barrel of oats, 6d. for wheat, 4d. for peas and the equivalent rate for barley. Sheep shearing was paid at the rate of 6½d. a day and a day's mowing was worth 10d.[5]

The services of tradesmen such as coopers, tailors, masons, chimney sweeps, and clock menders were also required from time to time. The accounts for 1779 record payment for nineteen shirts 'made for the master' and 'two pairs of breeches for Master Loftus', 'heel topping for the mistress', repair of the oven and 'turning and trimming chairs'. Some of these tradesmen were also cottiers in that they rented ground from the estate.[6]

The eighteenth-century estate papers make references to 'spalpeens', however, in numerical terms they were not a significant element in the community. Tim Ryan, Tom Toohy, John Harrington and Jack Doheny and Mick Bolan were the only people specifically identified as spalpeens in the three ledgers. Whether or not they were local people is unknown, as these surnames were not un-common in the district. A constabulary report in 1838 mentioned a Bryan

Page 'a Galway man who was labourer servant boy to Mr. Oakley of Castle Otway' and further mention was made of a John Collins 'a labourer who left the same employ to go to forest work with a man named Hodgins'.[7] Oakley was a tenant farmer and Hodgins combined farming with the job of wood ranger so it is possible that there was a greater number of spalpeens in the community but because they do not appear in the estate records they remain unknown to us.[8] Spalpeens were normally contracted to work for a specific period, so in a sense they had a certain degree of employment security. Mick Bolan was hired at the rate of £3 a year and was advanced 11s.4½d. to buy a coat.[9] John Harrington was engaged to work from November 1778 to April 1779. The big difference, from a community perspective, between cottiers and spalpeens, at least in the nineteenth-century, is that the latter were transient with no obvious stake in the community.

It is worthwhile to discuss the whole topic of leases in some detail, for a number of reasons. Recent research has focused on the landlord and tenant relationship in the mid-Victorian period or on larger estates such as the Downshire estates in counties Down and Wicklow which contained over 100,000 acres whereas this pamphlet covers the administration of a small estate of approximately 6,000 acres in the period before the Famine.[10] A series of acts were passed between 1704 and 1709 which limited Catholics' access to land, 'so that by 1778 scarcely 5 per cent of Irish land was left in Catholic hands'.[11] Thomas Power's study of eighteenth-century Tipperary, however, tracks the emergence of substantial Catholic head-tenants in south Tipperary, therefore, it is constructive to examine in detail the leasing policy of the Otway estate to get a perspective from the north of the county.[12] The lease was a significant tool of estate management, and here the leasing policy will be examined to ascertain its role in defining the socio-economic structure of the Castle Otway community, as it existed before the Famine of 1845.

In the eighteenth-century leases for land in Ireland were generally for a period of three named lives, usually the life of the lessee, his wife, son or sons, or for specific periods such as twenty-one or thirty-one years. Prior to the relief act of 1778 Catholics were not permitted to take leases for periods exceeding thirty-one years.[13] Observers of Irish agricultural life often included commentaries on the subject of leases with opinion divided as to whether leases were too long or too short. Ill-feeling between landlord and tenant was frequently attributed to insecurity of tenure. Long leases, so the argument went, were a hindrance to improvement, towards the end of a lease the tenant of a long lease was inclined to exhaust the land. On the other hand short leases discouraged tenants from investing in improvements.[14] The tenants in Glanaguile, were, according to the middleman Rev. Richard Lloyd, 'unwilling to attend their farms, though they had limestone, gravel and shell marl on the lands'. The reason he gave was 'the uncertainty of their tenure' even though 'all the leases are for three lives'.[15]

It is often overlooked that a lease was an agreement or contract between two parties. The terms and conditions under which a landlord was willing to let land and a tenant was equally willing to lease were binding upon the lessor and the lessee. The time at which a lease was made was a critical factor in establishing the provisions of a lease; the length, the annual rent, entry fine if any, restrictions on subletting and requirements to build or erect fences. A suitable tenant might be granted a long lease at an attractively low rent during periods of economic depression. In return for a high entry fine a cash-starved landlord might trade off the short term benefits from the fluctuations in agricultural prices for the security of a guaranteed annual income and thus offer a long lease at a low rent. When there was a shortage of land available for leasing and particularly if this coincided with a buoyant economy, the landlord could afford to demand a high rent and equally the tenant might be willing to pay a premium rent to secure a farm.[16]

A total of forty-four leases granted by the Otway estate between 1752 and 1808 have been traced and examined. Twenty leases were made before 1801 while the family was resident in Ireland. Henry Otway granted nineteen leases in 1801, and the remaining five were made, also by him, in 1808. During the eighteenth-century the leasing policy on the Otway estate operated within the law, leases for lives being granted to Protestants and leases for specific years to Catholics. By 1801 a significant change had taken place in the leasing policy of the estate, the religious denomination of the tenant was no longer the main criterion in determining the terms of a lease (table 2).

Of the twenty surviving leases made while the family was resident in Ireland, during the eighteenth-century, eleven leases for three lives were made between 1752 and 1773. The last lease for lives granted during this period was a lease for two lives to Charles MacDaniel, weaver, in 1773. In keeping with the law no leases for lives were granted to Catholic tenants on the Otway estate prior to the relief act of 1778.

Table 2. Religious composition of lease holders on the Otway estate 1752–87.

Terms	No of tenants	Religion
31 years	6	Catholic
30 years	1	Catholic
7 lives	1	Protestant
3 lives	10	Protestant
3 lives for ever	1	Protestant
2 lives	1	Protestant

Source: Otway estate papers, rent roll, 1806 NLI, MS 13000(8).

The practice of granting large tracts of land to head tenants who subse-
quentially sublet to under tenants at higher rents arose out of the Williamite
wars of the 1690s when large tracts of land were untenanted and there was a
need to attract solvent tenants. The landlord enjoyed a guaranteed income
from these lettings, the lessee in turn would sub-let the land in smaller lots at
higher rents for shorter periods to tenants who actually occupied and farmed
the land. During periods of sustained growth in the economy, such as during
the period 1770–1815, middlemen benefited, since many of the rents had been
fixed during years of economic difficulty and were consequently low.

During the eighteenth-century there was considerable representation of
Catholics at the level of middleman in County Tipperary, in spite of the
restrictions placed on their landholdings. McCarthy of Springfield, Keating of
Knockagh and Nagle of Garnvella were all substantial Catholic middlemen on
the Butler (Cahir) estates.[17] They were the dominant social and proprietorial
group in south Tipperary, while in the northern part of the county there were
few substantial Catholic head tenants. On the Otway estate eight lease holders
have been identified as middlemen, of whom only three can be positively
identified as Catholic; John Ryan of Garryglass and his widow and John
Lanigan who leased land in Glanaguile.[18] The latter was the only Catholic
with a significant holding but his lease was dated 1841, long after the relaxation
of the penal laws. Lanigan's lease was for 999 years and with terms like these
this transaction could be better described as an alienation of the land as
opposed to a leasing agreement.[19] Lanigan took over the agency of the Otway
estate following his brother's death in 1830 and continued in this position up
to 1841 and it is more than likely that because of this he was in a position to
lease the land.[20]

Two of the middlemen were related to the Otway family. Thomas Otway
leased 300 acres in Garrane to his brother James for a period of three lives,
renewable for ever.[21] A lease for seven lives was made, in 1758, to a John Lloyd
of Cranagh, near Nenagh, of land in Glanaguile. The reasons for these terms
are unclear, that Lloyd was distantly related to the Otway family may have been
a factor, the fact that the land in question was separated from the main body of
the Otway estate may also have influenced the terms of the agreement.[22] This
was also the largest tract of land leased by the estate, for over 700 acres.

Of the surviving thirteen leases for lives, only five were for land in excess
of one hundred acres: 102 acres, 260 acres, 300 acres, 440 acres and 700 acres
respectively. These four tenants, the head tenants or middlemen, John Short
and partner, James Otway, John Hunt together with John Lloyd made up the
layer of the socio-economic pyramid below the landlord. Short held two of
these leases.

Very little background information is available on the middlemen on the
Otway estate but what is known helps form an understanding of the attitudes
and activities of this group of people. An advertisement placed by John Lloyd

of Glanaguile in the *Clonmel Gazette* in 1789 gives some indication of the resources commanded by some middlemen. Lloyd announced that he had '300 bullocks and 4–600 two to four year old sheep for sale at the fair of Borrisoleigh'.[23] In November of the same year he advertised the letting of part of the lands of Glanaguile which was described as '200 acres of good sheep walk ... with excellent marl on the land ... a large barn and a good dwelling house'.[24]

By 1828 Rev. Richard Lloyd, then living in Devon, was quite anxious to surrender his lease of Glanaguile to the Otway estate as his two sons, one of whom was in the navy and the other in the church, had no interest in it. He was of the opinion that

> should you wish to dispossess the present tenants there are but five or six who may not be evicted at the quarter sessions, neither do I believe any of them would give you much trouble.[25]

George Fawcett took over the lands in Garrane leased originally by James Otway and Fawcett was described in a report in the *Tipperary Vindicator* as 'a good landlord'. It was reported, in the Famine year of 1847, that Fawcett on receiving his rents from his numerous tenantry in the neighbourhood of Castle Otway, Toomevara and Moneygall gave an abatement of 25 per cent 'though he let his lands at moderate rents.'[26] In addition he cancelled all arrears for those who wished to go to America and 'allowed them the full benefit of tenant right by selling their interest to the best and fairest bidder'.[27] Furthermore he also assisted tenants in paying their passage to America. This contrasts with another report in the same newspaper where the correspondent from Borrisoleigh in describing the destitution of the people castigated the middle men of the locality 'who are exacting by the most stringent courses what they call their rights' and were issuing writs and ejectments where rents were outstanding, despite the fact 'some of them were owing two years' rent themselves'.[28]

Seven leases for three lives have survived and these were offered to Protestant tenant farmers whose descendants continued to farm in the area well into the nineteenth-century. With the exception of two leases which were for part of the townlands of Curreeny and of Knockfune, all these leaseholders had property which was close to the heart of the estate, and they formed a ring, as it were, of Protestant tenants around the demesne. These farms varied in size from fourteen acres in Killederdadrum to fifty acres in Roan, with rents working out at about 10s. an acre. The two leases for land on the perimeter of the estate were made to one individual, a James Lee. The land in Knockfune was then in the possession of an Andrew Ryan, gentleman, and presumably James Lee sublet these lands, the terms of which are unknown.[29] During the term of Thomas Otway's ownership of the estate (died 1786) the freeholder tenants with farms under 100 acres accounted for not more than 350 acres and for approximately £100 of the estate's annual income. The annual overall return from leased land was around £700 at a time when the income of the estate was estimated at £2,000.[30]

From a list of freeholders of County Tipperary, dated 1776, eight freeholders have been identified by virtue of their leasing Otway land; Stephen Lloyd, Cooke Otway, Loftus Otway, Bamlet and Joshua Wright who had leases for three lives, as did James Lee and Leonard Shouldice.[31] The only freeholder for whom a lease has not been discovered was Alex Caldwell of Nelson Hall, who was steward under Thomas Otway. In 1793 the parliamentary franchise was widened to include in the county electorate Catholic leaseholders for lives. These became known as the forty-shilling freeholders.[32] This change in the legislation was used by politically active landlords to grant leases to tenants which would qualify them for the vote. However, as the leases on the Otway estate which fell into this category, forty-shilling freeholds, were not made until 1801, at a time when the landlord was living in England, it is difficult to ascribe a political motive to the granting of these particular leases.

The extent to which the Otways influenced their tenants who had the franchise is difficult to establish as only one specific reference has been found. During the election campaign of Nicholas Maher of Turtulla, Thurles, in 1844, Robert Otway Cave wrote to the *Tipperary Vindicator*, the newspaper associated with repeal, saying that he intended writing to 'my agent to have in readiness all those votes with whom I may have any influence and to give you every assistance in his power'.[33] Nicholas Maher was identified with the repeal movement and was the nephew of Valentine Maher who with Otway Cave was successful in the election of 1841 at the expense of two conservative candidates.[34]

Between 1752–87 seven leases were made for specified number of years, one for thirty years and six for thirty-one years. These lessees had surnames which were and still are very common in this area and in all probability these tenants were Catholics. The single thirty-year lease was made by Cooke Otway to a partnership of four farmers in the townland of Tooreigh. The lease, dated May 1787, was for ninety-five acres with an annual rent of £47.12s.10d.[35] A second partnership lease, for thirty-one years and dated 1772, has survived. The partners to this lease were Tim, Martin and John Ryan of Coolicarra, in Curreeny.[36] The granting of leases to farmers in partnership was an option open to landlords when there was a shortage of suitable tenants. For these tenants it was a means by which they gained access to land which might not have been possible were they to farm independently. Partnership farming did not always run smoothly as the recommendation made by the agent Thomas Ryder Pepper in 1823 suggests, the

> accounts of this townland [Tooreigh] being extremely confused and none of the tenants being able to pay their arrears it is recommended to set the entire in one farm to a sufficiently solvent tenant.[37]

John Ryan of Garryglass, who held three of the six thirty-one year leases, is an interesting case study of a leasee. Some of the details of his life can be pieced together from the estate records. In 1772 his account was headed 'John Ryan Steward'.[38] The half yearly rent of his one third share of the tillage in Garryglass was £1. He also had a third share of meadowing also in Garryglass. The half yearly rent of this meadow of two acres three roods was 18s.9d. He also rented a farm in Lackenavourna, the annual rent of which was £6.12s.9d.[39] By 1778 he had moved up the social and economic ladder, he was now described as 'John Ryan Esq.' His holdings now included land in Gortnaskehy, Coolicarra, Knockavoga and Knockfune. The total annual rent for all his lands was now £21.17s.9d.[40] The quantity of land involved varied from five acres in Coolicarra to 151 acres in Knockavoga.[41]

Some of the lands were occupied by other people at the time of the granting of these leases to John Ryan. The farm at Coolicarra was in the possession of a Denis Ryan, that in Knockfune was occupied by a Patrick McLoughney.[42] John Ryan in turn sublet the twenty-nine acres in Knockfune to the occupier at a rent of £4 per annum, while his own rent was £1 a year.[43] The rent of the land in Gortnaskehy which cost Ryan 10s. a year was leased to the occupier, Thomas Kennedy, in 1776 at an annual rent of £1.10s.0d. Both of these sub-leases, to the sitting tenants, were to run for thirty-one years and were made with the landlord's permission.

What was the nature of the relationship between John Ryan and the landlord Thomas Otway? Is he to be regarded as an eighteenth-century anchor tenant? In return for land at favourable rents was he to encourage others to settle in these areas and thus bring the land into use? Much of the land rented by Ryan was in Curreeny and the tenant input into the reclamation of marginal lands in this townland was very well described by Fr. Glynn, curate of Killeen, Templederry, in 1870,

> the tenants live about eleven miles from Nenagh the nearest market town . . . the nearest lime kiln was eight miles distant. Having bought the lime in most cases they has to take it on their backs to the mountain to be reclaimed.[44]

The Otway estate acquired Garryglass, by lease, in 1772. A map of the townland, dated at this time, shows a nucleated settlement described as 'the village'. Also shown on the map was Tom Kennedy's part of the mountain

> on which he has expended much labour and capital, having made 2 ½ acres of meadow, 4 acres of arable or pasture or meadow, 6 acres of good grass and 7 ½ acres of mountain.[45]

Thus it may be possible to explain why the steward John Ryan was granted
leases in this townland. He continued working as steward. Between November
1778 and 1779 he worked for 308 days for which he was owed £12.16s.8d.
and he was allowed a rebate of his rent for one of his farm on account of his
being occupied with 'the master's business'.[46] His relationship with the landlord
and his economic and social position within the estate community made him
a suitable intermediary between this newly acquired property and the outside
world. John Ryan was in the position to regulate internal customary practices of
this micro-community and represent the community to the outside world.[47]

John Ryan's account with the estate reveals the wide range of income-
generating activities in which he was involved. Besides the rental income from
subletting land and his wages from the estate, Ryan also made money from
supplying yarn: '14 doz of yarn spun' made him 3s., over a hundredweight of
butter yielded £2.4s.0d. and he was paid 3s. for wild fowl and hares 'at sundry
times'.[48] It is not clear from these financial records what was the extent of
Ryan's involvement in the domestic woollen industry and butter making. Did
he only supply the castle or was he involved in the wider trade? Did he
produce the goods himself or was his role that of distribution agent? If his role
was that of butter factor how important was the butter trade to the local
economy? John Ryan, furthermore, seemed to have acted as a local banker of
sorts. The records disclose the indebtedness of other tenants to him, Joseph
Wright owed £5.15s.0d., Tom Twohey 10s.0d., and Pat Collins £5.15s.0d.
Orders for these amounts were offset by the estate against the amount of rent
due from Ryan's rent.[49] There are no pointers as to the circumstances in
which these debts were incurred.

Julian Ryan or Widow Ryan of Garryglass was the other person to whom
a thirty-one year lease was granted; the source of this information is the 1806
rent roll where it was noted that the lease was made in November 1784. The
annual rent was £24.11s.0d., the quantity of land involved was not specified.[50]
This woman was more than likely the widow of the aforementioned John
Ryan of Garryglass. Two deeds which have survived among the Otway estate
papers in England confirm that the practice of sub-letting land to partnerships
continued in Curreeny into the nineteenth-century. In January 1805 Julian
Ryan of Garryglass, described as 'gentlewoman' leased part of the lands of
Knockfune containing twenty-nine acres then in her tenure to John
McLoughney, Thomas McLoughney, Sen., Thomas McLoughney Jun., and
Edmond Mulcahy, all farmers from Knockfune, at £10 per annum for a period
of thirty-one years.[51] The following month she leased part of the lands of
Gortnaskehy containing sixteen acres at £2.5s.6d. a year to a group of farmers;
Thomas Kennedy Jun., Thomas Kennedy Sen. and Andrew Kennedy. On this
occasion the lease was to run for twenty-three years. These new rents were
higher than the rents of 1776 when the lands had been originally sub-let by

John Ryan, then the rent to the sub-tenant of Gortnaskehy was £1 per annum and that of Knockfune £4.[52]

While the Ryans were not in the same league as the lessees who leased land in excess of 100 acres or even entire townlands, they were nonetheless middlemen. They sublet to subordinate tenants at higher rents, John Ryan's own rent for Knockfune was £1 a year while his sub-tenants paid him four times that amount. Ryan's rent was 10s. a year for Gortnaskehy, while the rent charged to the sub-tenants was £1. The Ryans provide an interesting contrast to the Catholic head-tenants portrayed by Power in his study of eighteenth-century Tipperary. The activities of the Scully family of Kilfeacle help to make this point. Their leased land grew from 2,000 acres in 1776, to 4,000 acres in 1792 and to 6,000 acres by 1803. Much of this land was by 1803 held by lease for three lives. In 1792 they stocked about 1,500 of the 4,000 acres and sub-let the remainder at a profit.[53]

In the last years of the eighteenth-century when agricultural prices were rising the general tendency was towards granting shorter leases.[54] The Otway estate rent rolls dating from 1806, reflect this trend. Furthermore by the early years of the new century a fundamental change had taken place in the management and exploitation of the estate, a development which was crucial in altering the economic structure of the community. The landlord, Henry Otway, was now resident in England and this could be regarded as the catalyst for this change. The Otway family no longer farmed on its own account, the income from the estate was, hereafter, primarily rental income. Arising from this alteration in the exploitation of the estate, there was no longer the same demand for farm labour which had existed in the eighteenth-century, and as more land became available for renting, the tenant farmer became the predominant class within the community.

It is difficult to pinpoint exactly when this alteration in the socio-economic structure took place. There are some indications that perhaps the family was in the process of withdrawing from direct involvment in farming by 1793 when an estate map dated for that year shows parcels of land quite close to the demesne in the hands of tenant farmers. The names of the divisions may indicate that they were once part of the demesne: Ryefield, Limekiln field, Cow Park, Clover meadow, Oatfield.[55] Some of these tenancies were partnership ventures; one holding is listed as belonging to Abraham Harrington and partners and another to Edmund Finn and partners. These were more than likely tenancies at will, since the first leases for these farms are dated 1801. There were probably always tenants at will on the estate but they are first clearly identified as a separate category in the rent roll of 1806 (table 3).

Seventy-one tenants were listed in the 1806 rental, of whom twenty-four were tenants at will, twenty-nine had leases for the life of the lessee. The remaining eighteen tenants, with five exceptions, had old leases. The exceptions were Adam Hodgins who had part of Knockfune as salary for 'attending

Killavalla wood' and Rev. Edmund Jourdan who rented his land in Templederry 'during his incumbency'.[56] The terms of two tenancies were unspecified. All of the leases made during Henry Otway's ownership of the estate were for the life of the lessee, save one lease, made in May 1801, between the landlord and Leonard Shouldice for seven acres of land in Lackenavourna for the lives of Leonard and his youngest son William.[57] Sixteen of the twenty-nine leases for one life have been traced, only one of which was registered in the Registry of Deeds. The leases were dated 11 May 1801 and were made between Henry Otway of Stanford Hall, Leicester and the tenants who were already in occupation of the lands. The time lapse between these new leases and Henry Otway's inheriting the estate was only six months thus it would seem that this was a new policy under a new landlord.

There is no obvious reason as to why some tenants were granted leases for life and others were tenants at will. Tenants at will were to be found side by side with those who had a life interest in their farms. A tenant could have a life interest in one property and be a tenant at will in another as was the case with Abraham Harrington. He had a lease for a life in Scalespoint for sixty-acres while he was a tenant at will in The Felix Wood where he had thirty-eight acres. While it is impossible to be absolutely certain as to religious denomination, Protestant tenants and Catholic tenants were to be found among the tenants at will. John Mooney had thirty-seven acres rented in Glantane as had John and Nicholas Shouldice, all three were tenants at will. Approximately a third of the tenants at will were Protestant (based on the evidence of surnames) and the same ratio had leases for life.

Table 3. Profile of leases on the Otway estate 1806

Terms	No of leases
Lease for life	29
at will	24
3 lives	8
2 lives	2
31 years	2
7 lives	1
3 lives for ever	1
In lieu of salary as wood ranger	1
To run during the incumbency of the rector	1
Unspecified	1
Total	**70**

Source: Otway estate papers rent roll 1806, NLI MS 13000(8)

The rent roll of 1806 shows that 1,992 acres were now directly leased to tenant farmers and this generated an annual income of £2,154. Tenants at will farmed 584 acres and generated £757 in rental income for the estate, at an average of £1.29 per acre. Rental income from the tenants with leases for life amounted to £1,167 and involved 837 acres, the average rent per acre was £1.39. In contrast the head tenants or middlemen leased 1,745 acres producing an income of £527.[58] Tenants with old leases, including the middlemen, accounted in total for 2,309 acres of the estate and contributed £718 annually to the estate which works out at approximately £0.31 per acre. The difference in the terms of tenure may have originated with the economic boom in agriculture which the country experienced up to 1815. This practice of mixing leases for life and tenancies at will guaranteed the landlord a certain annual income from the tenants for life and provided a safeguard against a decrease in agricultural prices while allowing him a degree of flexibility in setting the rents of the tenants at will in line with prevailing economic conditions and thus benefiting from any increase in the value of agricultural produce.[59]

In the rent roll of 1806 three widows were each described as tenants at will indicating a general shift in estate management away from leases for life to tenancies at will.[60] At a time when the long term trend on the Otway estate was away from leases to tenancies at will, leases for three lives were still being granted on the middleman property of Glanaguile as late as 1818 and 1820.[61] By 1834 all of the leases for one life had expired on the Otway estate with the exception of Abraham Harrington's lease of Scalespoint.[62] In 1853 there were only two leases in existence. The original Fawcett lease for three lives renewable for ever was renewed in 1831 and John Lanigan's lease as previously mentioned, dated from 1841.[63]

In addition to the rental terms, a lease might contain other contractual obligations, requirements to ditch, hedge and manure the land and the use of the land.[64] A representative sample from the Otway estate papers follows. Thomas Lee in Middleplough was to enclose the land with ditches and plant with quicks on pain of a £30 penalty.[65] Penalties for subletting could be quite severe. Adam Hodgins was liable to an extra £10 a year on his rent if he sublet the land.[66] Michael Oakley's lease of 1801 restricted land in tillage to six acres a year.[67] The lessees of land in Lackenavourna were not permitted to keep goats as they were considered to pose a threat to young plantations.[68] One unusual regulation which was inserted in some of the late-eighteenth-century agreements was the clause which required the tenant to rear a whelp annually, if required. In 1794 James and William Lee indicated in a letter that they wished to surrender their lease of Nelson Hall because they found the stipulation which obliged them to rear a hound or pay £3 in lieu, too onerous.[69]

The withdrawal of the Otway family from direct exploitation of their estate impacted heavily on the cottiers and labourers as there was very little regular general labouring work available on the estate from 1801 onwards. The rent rolls for 1823 and 1825 contain details of wages paid by the estate and from these it is possible to monitor the decline in employment opportunities on the estate. The wages bill for 1823 came to £396 and that for 1825 to £260.[70] The nature of the employment, was moreover quite, specific. Matt Collins and company supplied turf to the castle, Thomas Dagg was due three years' salary for surveying at Lissenhall, Adam Hodgins was employed as part time driver while Bulger received a salary for acting as steward and for 'horse work'.[71] Furthermore the farm labourer and cottier had to compete with the tenant farmer for whatever work was available, particularly during periods of acute distress. In the early 1820s, which were difficult years, several of the larger tenants found employment on the plantations at Castle Otway, John Ryan of Oatfield, who worked at 'barking' had thirty-three acres.[72] Ebby Harrington, who had twenty-nine acres, broke stones for the new road at Loughane during the famine year of 1848.[73]

Landlords, it has been argued, were encouraged to subdivide their property into small holdings by the changes in the electoral law of 1793 which enfranchised Catholics and the subdivision of land also increased their rental income.[74] When the property qualification for electoral franchise was raised to £10 in 1829, these 40s. freeholders ceased to be desirable and evictions followed. The division of land among children on marriage was another contributory factor to rural poverty. By examining the rent rolls it is possible to see to what extent farms were subdivided on the Otway estate (table 4).

Based on three rent rolls which detail acreage, the median size farm ranged from twenty-three to twenty acres, during the period 1806–34.[75] Again during

Table 4. Number of holdings on the Otway estate, according to size

Size of holdings	1806	1827	1834	Mean for 3 years
Unknown	7	25	2	11.33
Under 1 acre	0	0	1	0.33
1–5	6	2	10	6
5–15	8	7	30	15
15–30	23	22	48	31
30–50	13	13	24	16.6
50–100	6	13	8	9
100–200	4	4	4	4
200–500	3	3	3	3
above 500	1	1	0	0.67
Total	**71**	**90**	**130**	**96.93**

Source: Otway estate papers rent rolls, NLI MS 13000(3), Mortgage deeds NA D20386, D.20387

the same period the modal farm size was fifteen and thirty acres, that is more tenants had farms in this range than in any other. In 1806, twenty-three tenants had farms which ranged between fifteen and thirty acres, in 1827 the number was twenty-two, in 1834 the figure rose to forty-eight farms. The corresponding percentages for the years 1806, 1827, 1834 were 32 per cent, 33.8 per cent, 36.9 per cent respectively.

The total number of holdings increased over the period through a degree of subdivision and also through old leases falling in and the former tenants of middlemen holding directly from the estate. By 1834 the seven-life-lease of Glanaguile had been surrendered by the middleman Rev. Richard Lloyd in return for a yearly annuity of £300. This surrender added approximately thirty-four tenants to the number of direct tenants.[76] The increase in the number of direct tenants did not significantly alter the pattern of landholding on the estate as can be seen from the chart which illustrates the average of farm size over the three specific years of 1806, 1827 and 1834.

There are several aspects of land tenure on the Otway estate which the statistical tables conceal. The tables of farm size could be said to misrepresent the average farm size because there was no distinction made between the occupiers of single holdings and those farmers who had more than one holding. Abraham Harrington is a good example of a farmer with more than one holding. In 1816 he had three separate holdings, in 1819 he had four and by 1827 his holding consisted of his original sixty acres farm. The thirty-eight acres which he had rented in The Felix were now in the possession of Caleb Powell.[77] There were several partnership farms on the estate. John and James Stapleton farmed forty-nine acres in Knockfune in 1827 and while the

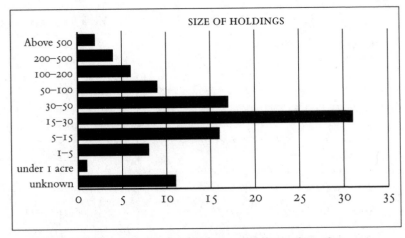

4. Mean farm size for the three years 1806, 1827, 1834
Source: Otway estate papers NLI, MS 13000(8), NA, D20386, D 20387

holding was above the median size farm, two people, if not two families, had to make a living from the farm. Several of the earlier partnership farms seem to have been between people who were unrelated. The Bulger and Lee joint tenancy in 1819 and that of Ackland and Hogan in 1820 would be representative of this type of joint venture.[78] By the later period this practice of non-kinship partnership farming was dying out and partnership farming seems to have been confined to people who were related.

Calculating holdings in terms of acres does not take account of the quality of land. One of the first official country-wide valuations of property was Griffiths' Valuation, on the Primary Valuation is more popularly known. The first surveyors started working in Templederry in August 1845. The Primary Valuation is a useful gauge of the quality of agricultural land, as the valuation was to be based on an agreed average price for agricultural produce. The valuations placed on land on the Otway estate varied from 12s. per acre in Falleeny to 1s.6d. per acre in Curreeny. The rent rolls would suggest that the pattern of land holding was a concentration of farms above the median size in the higher value townlands. Honoria Ryan, widow, rented ninety-eight acres in Falleeny, the townland with the highest value. In Cloghonan, a townland with a valuation of 10s.5d. per acre, three of the five farms there were above sixty acres.

In Curreeny, which was described by the Ordnance Survey as a 'large townland very partially cultivated, being chiefly composed of rough boggy land . . . Coolicarra village is in the west side near the centre, Knockfune village is in the south east side.' the average valuation of land was 1s.6d. per acre.[79] In the adjoining townland of Garryglass it was 2s.6d. per acre. The pattern of land holding in these marginal townlands contrasted with the primarily single family occupancy of holdings in the high value townlands. The manuscript field books of the Primary Survey depict a confusion of shares and portions of holdings in these poorer townlands. One such holding of seventy-eight acres and valued at about £19 was divided between William Ryan whose share was 5/24ths, Martin Ryan's was 3/16ths, Thomas Kennedy's was 5/24ths, James Kennedy had 5/24ths, James Butler, the same and finally Pat Coffey had a garden.[80] This practice of subdivision which resulted in microscopic farms appears to have been largely confined to these two areas; Garryglass and Curreeny. The Primary Valuation also reveals a high proportion of surnames in common indicating kinship links between the occupiers of land in these townlands. These townlands have many of the characteristics associated with *clachans*, or rundale villages; nucleated groups of farmhouses, land holding communally organised and bonds of kinship between the inhabitants.[81] The Harrington farm in Shanballyard which was subdivided by 1845, three brothers each had a one third share of 'the good and the bad land . . . as in Curreeny', stands out as an anomaly. That this was regarded as a peculiarity associated with poorer areas of the parish is underscored by folk memory.[82]

The evidence from the rent rolls is very much in favour of arguing that the pressure of population and the accompanying demand for land was relieved by the utilisation of land which had previously been under used and in the peripheral areas of the estate. The farms in Lackenavourna were described as 'improved since taken by reclaiming the hill'.[83] The fact that by 1834 it was considered necessary and worthwhile to survey and measure the holdings in the two townlands of Garryglass and Curreeny is a strong indication that these marginal areas had been brought into cultivation and were now a source of income to the estate. The tenants in Curreeny were listed as Larry Ryan with fifty acres, John Ryan Keeper with sixty-six acres while Thomas Ryan and company had thirty-eight acres, previously the extent of these holdings had not been specified.[84]

Another strategy adopted to relieve the pressure of population on the land was emigration. There are some references, in the rentals, to tenants going to America. Andrew Kennedy of Tooreigh was one such tenant.[85] The Church of Ireland bishop of Killaloe and Kilfenora requested information from his clergy on conditions in the parishes. The questionnaire is dated 1820, and several clergymen noted the emigration of Protestant families to America and Canada.[86] The previously mentioned Rev. Studdert also noted, in 1835, that there was some emigration to America from his parish.[87] An indication of the costs involved in emigration is given by an advertisement in the *Nenagh Gazette*. While there was free passage to Australia for married agricultural servants and single women, single men in the age group eighteen to thirty had to pay £5, the cost for a child of free parents was £4.[88] Emigrants had to provide themselves with a box, a knife, fork, several spoons, a metal plate, a hook pot and a half pint drinking pot. In addition they had to defray their own travel costs to Dublin or Cork and to provide their own food. With costs like this emigration was not an option for everyone. Emigration and the greater utilisation of poorer and waste lands relieved congestion to some extent on the Otway estate in the pre-Famine period so that sub-division did not reach such dangerous proportions as it it did elsewhere in Ireland.

The estate records, however, deal only with direct tenants. Under tenants or cottiers do not feature. The survey team employed for carrying out the Primary Valuation worked on Templederry in August 1845 and the manuscript field and house books show a high correlation between these early records and the printed valuation in terms of occupiers. The manuscript field books for the townland of Ballyphillip, near Nenagh, and part of the Otway Lissenhall estate described some tenants as Mrs. Dagg's 'cottier tenants'.[89] There are no such references in the Templederry field books leading to the conclusion that such cottier tenants were few on the main Otway estate. The evidence of the poor law rate books for the parish of Templederry reinforces the impression that cottiers did not compose a significant element in the Otway estate community in nineteenth-century.[90] The Otway estate as landlord was not liable to pay the poor rate rate for significant numbers of tenants.

Some aspects of the movements in the rental income of the estate can be studied from the estate records and it is indisputable that the anticipated rental income dropped from its highest level of £3,190 in 1813 to £2,562 in 1852. The impact of the cessation of hostilities in Europe following the battle of Waterloo in 1815 had an immediate and dramatic impact on demand for Irish agricultural produce and this was reflected not only in the landlord's income but also in the inability of tenants to meet their rents, underscoring the integration of the local economy of Castle Otway with the national and continental economies (table 5).[91]

At the level of the individual tenant, Abraham Harrington of Scalespoint is a good example of the consequences of the severe deflation following the battle of Waterloo. Up to 1815 Abraham Harrington who leased sixty acres at an annual rent of £96 and an additional thirty-eight acres in the Felix Wood at a rent of £78 was able to meet his rental commitments. By 1816 he had built up arrears of £68, in May he only paid £28 of his half yearly rental and arrears due in November 1816 were £129. Arrears in May 1819 stood at £159, in November 1819 these had grown to £180, £228 in 1820, £438 in 1823 and in 1825 the arrears on his holding at Scalespoint alone was £129. He had to surrender his holding in 'The Felix' in 1827.[92]

Table 5. Rental income and arrears on the Otway estate 1806–52

Year	Arrears due since last	Rent	Paid (half year)	Arrears due
1806	N/A	£2681 *	N.A	N/A
1811	£61	£1597 **	£1579	£79
1813	£151	£1595 **	£1568	£178
1816	£409	£1431 **	£660	£1179
1819	£1412	£2706 *	£2585	£1534
1820	£1668	£3355 ***	£2925	£2098
1823	£1728	£7643 ****	£5529 **	£3460
1825	£1896	£2740 *	£2658	£1718
1827		£2766 *	N/A	N/A
1834		£2690 *		N/A
1852		£2562 *		N/A

Source: Otway estate rentals (NA, LEC 25/20; NLI, MS 13000(8); LCA 23/57/1030) (* yearly rent, ** half year's rent, *** includes rents due in May 1820 and Nov 1820, **** three years' rent due and paid)

How did landlords react to the inability of tenants to pay their rents? A variety of solutions to the problem of arrears were adopted by landlords, eviction, rent reduction and distraint of goods.[93] Examples of these solutions are found in the Otway estate papers confirming the findings of recent research, namely that tenants were not evicted at will but only after due legal process. The landlord had to balance his costs of an eviction against the loss of the tenant's arrears. In the rent roll of 1818 John Maloney was noted as being under notice to quit, and again in 1820 he was still under 'ejectment'. Patrick and James Donovan were to be 'ejected at the July sessions' in Nenagh. Maloney's arrears were £18 while those of the Donovans were £66. John and James Stapleton were to pay their arrears of £178 or else quit. Tim Costello was 'to be removed' if his arrears of £31 were not paid whereas Michael Kennedy was to pay one third of his arrears.[94] Several tenants had their rents reduced, Roger Ryan's rent was reduced from 20s. an acre to 14s. an acre, Charles Canny was given a quarter reduction of his rent. The agent observed that the tenants in Tooreagh 'all require an abatement as they cannot pay the growing rent much less their arrears.' There is one record of seizure of stock, stock was seized from Abraham Harrington's farm, in 1823.

The picture which emerges from this study of the tenantry on the Otway estate thus is not of a homogeneously structured society. While the records chart the emergence of the tenant farmer as the predominant social and economic class on the estate, there were differences within this section in terms of access to resources. On the theme of landlord and tenant relations, the tenantry would appear to be have been more at the mercy of the wider economy than of a capricious landlord who raised rents and evicted tenants on a whim. The wider economy has to be viewed as of part of the loop which bound the landlord and tenants together.

The Community

In this chapter the Castle Otway community is observed as a system or a web of connected people, all of whom affected each other. By examining the dynamic interaction or interdependence of these people it will be very apparent that this specific community was part of a wider system.

The family is fundamental to social organisation and in the period before the direct involvement by central agencies, whether public or private, in the provision of education and social welfare, the family was not only a social unit but an economic one, a welfare unit, and the primary educator of future generations in practical as well as spiritual and social matters. Women in particular had a direct relevance to the structure of the community in the past

> Women helped to maintain social attitudes, to foster a sense of communal identity and to transmit these to the next generation. Women were the keepers of the communal memory, and the holders of local and family consciousness.[1]

Already some facets of the dynamics of this group have been touched on, the membership of the group itself and the role of the landlord as agent of change particularly in shaping the group structure and as agricultural innovator. In so far as the evidence allows other aspects will be investigated: group cohesion, interpersonal conflict, conflict resolution, leadership and the integration of the community in the wider world.

Unfortunately very little is known of family life in pre-Famine Templederry. The sequences of parish registers of the two religious communities are not sufficiently long for any meaningful conclusions to be drawn.[2] Was the family life experience of the Otway estate community different from other communities, at parish level or at a national level? How different was the range of experiences of people categorised as farmers and cottiers? Were there class differences in the geographical spread of marriage partners? The parish registers give some indication, at least for the post-Famine period, that members of the Protestant community were more likely to find partners from outside their parish and from a wider catchment area. This is not surprising considering that some of the Protestant tenant farmers were relatively recent incomers to the parish and thus would have ties with other areas. The names Carter, Ackland and Markby all appear in the rent rolls for the first time in 1813, Bulger in 1825, Powell in

1827.[3] In what other ways were the similar life experiences different between Catholics and Protestants?

By synthesising the evidence from the estate records and from life histories of individuals some comments can be made on the role of the family and the importance of kinship. The family transmitted the skills which led to effective independent performance in the larger economic system. Fathers and sons often worked together on their own farms or on the estate. Entries such as 'Paddy Gleeson and son' and 'John Hardy saddler and boy', 'Pat Donovan and son carpenter', 'Roger Ryan and sons' appeared regularly in the ledgers.[4] Daniel Ryan 'herd' and sons rented the grass of six cows and one horse and three acres of garden in 1780, while Thomas McLoughney Senior and Junior were in partnership in Knockfune in 1805.[5] Dennis Hanley's girl worked for seventeen days at the rate of 17*d*. per day for Mrs. Otway. The fact that the wages of offspring were included with the fathers' is an indication that delayed entry into autonomous adult life was, for some people, a feature of family life. The role of women in the weaving and spinning on the Otway estate and their contribution to the family income has been previously noted. There was, incidentally a lower value placed on women's work, they were paid apparently at the same rate as boys. There was also a category of unspecified work described in the records as 'women's work', with no indication as to whether these women were cottiers or tenant farmers, their wives, sisters or daughters.[6]

The importance of kinship links in the community, as far as participation in the rituals of life is concerned, have been graphically described by a local historian who wrote of the people of Curreeny streaming out of their homes bearing their dead to their ancestral burial places of Latteragh and Ballinaclough.[7] How important was kinship in daily life? The support of the extended family was crucial in an era when public charity was unstructured; the dispensary system, for example was only introduced in 1803. In his submission to the poor law inquiry, in 1835, the rector of Latteragh, Mr. Studdert, stated that while there were very few deserted children in the parish, those who were deserted lived with friends. About eighty widows were supported by friends or their children. Those, 'impotent through age', supported themselves by begging or 'their children and friends'.[8]

The solidarity between neighbours in the Irish countryside, whether for economic or practical reasons, manifested itself in the *meitheal*, where neighbours came together to harvest and trash each others crops, save hay and turf, sharing manpower and tools.[9] The Otway estate, even under the control of an absentee landlord, provided many opportunities for neighbours to come together as working parties, whether working on the land together, drawing sand or turf, going to the fair or to Limerick for coal for the castle. The account books log expenses incurred in going to fairs, for example payment for three men going to the fair at Borrisoleigh and three men at the fair of Holy Cross.[10] From the earlier records we get an appreciation of what bound neighbours together, there were instances of neighbourly indebtedness which crossed class and religious lines. The role of John Ryan of Garryglass as a local banker has already been described. The difficulties in obtaining credit in the 1840s, an age of underdeveloped banking systems, were detailed by James Jocelyn Poe, agent to Lord Orkney in the adjoining parish of Latteragh, in his evidence to the Devon commission. In describing Hayes' bank in Portroe, Nenagh, Poe stated that a tenant had no business asking for a renewal of a loan

> unless he spend 1s. in the house on whisky or coffee and he has besides to treat his two bails men which costs him 9d. to 1s. more every three months.[11]

Economic ties and practical co-operation would have been cemented by social ties, whether by the *cuairdíocht* at night or other gatherings of a social nature.[12]

Notwithstanding these ties, it would be a mistake to see this community as untouched by interpersonal conflict. The fact that neighbours may also have been relatives was no guarantee of peaceful co-existence. Indeed when this group, the Castle Otway community, came under official scrutiny, it was characterised by strife. An indication of the extent of lawlessness in the wider community generally is implicit, for example, in the analyses of indictable crimes in the spring assizes in Nenagh in 1844. Of seventy-three people sent for trial in north Tipperary twenty-two were charged with murder, three with conspiracy and thirteen for assaulting habitations by night.[13] Reports of assaults on the person and on property are to be found in the correspondence between the local constabulary, stationed in Castle Otway and in Garryglass, with the Chief Secretary's office in Dublin Castle.

The following cases are representative of the type of activities which were classified by the police as outrages. The house of a 'respectable man named Harrington', between Castle Otway and Borrisoleigh was attacked by some armed men who 'totally demolished the doors and windows', according to a report in the *Dublin Packet* in August 1838. The accuracy of this report was challenged in the official report to Dublin Castle, the respectable farmer 'is a poor labourer' and 'not a single window in the miserable hut' was broken.[14] In September of the same year, 1838, William Ryan of Gortnagoona was waylaid on the way home from the fair at Castle Otway by 'John Collins of Castle Otway and two other persons with stones'.[15] Eight sheep, the property of John Cleary of Garrane were fleeced and the constable making the report commented that 'this part of the county where this outrage has taken place is infested with sheep stealers'.[16]

In 1836 Launcelot Costello, a servant at Castle Otway, was sentenced to transportation for life for manslaughter.[17] Ten years later another servant at the castle, a wood ranger named Timothy Hanley was murdered, an event which

Mrs. Otway Cave referred to in a letter to her solicitor as 'Poor Tim Hanly's dreadful end'.[18] The contrasting newspaper reports reveal internal community tensions which are often over-shadowed by the landlord-tenant relationship. The *Tipperary Vindicator* covered the murder of Tim Hanley in depth when it reported in its edition of 9 October 1847 that

> Timothy Hanley, an honest man employed as caretaker by Mrs. Otway Cave was shot dead by some assassin as he was preparing to go to bed, we heard of no cause for this truly diabolical murder.

The edition of the paper for 13 October carried the story with the headline 'horrible murder at Castle Otway'. The paper eulogised Hanley in the following terms

> There were few more intelligent persons of his class than Tim Hanley. He was exceedingly well read in the details of Irish history and was a good scholar also. In his earlier days he was a wild reckless mountaineer, often engaged in faction fighting, the disgrace and ruin of the country, but he sobered down in latter years under the benign influence of temperance and enjoyed a sufficiency with the good esteem of the princely lady who owns Castle Otway.[19]

The *Nenagh Guardian* was not quite so fulsome in praising Timothy Hanley in its report of the murder.

> In his [Hanley's] younger days he was either the head of or connected with a notorious faction which existed in Castle Otway some years ago. So much had the people in the vicinity of Castle Otway been afraid of him, that none of them would attempt to touch any portion of the property over which he had been caretaker.[20]

That such a character became Mrs. Otway Cave's caretaker poses some questions. Was he employed to coerce people to behave through fear? Or was Mrs. Otway Cave, who appeared to be genuinely distressed by Hanley's murder, partly motivated by a desire to rehabilitate him.

Several local people were suspected of involvement in the crime. At the inquest, James Bourke of Cloghinch claimed, as part of his evidence, that 'Hanley said he had enemies in Robert Chambers and Patrick Donovan'.[21] Chambers was the steward at the castle and Donovan was possibly a farmer from Clashbeg.[22] Other people came under suspicion as a letter from Mrs. Otway Cave to her agent indicates. 'I am glad' she wrote, that the Waddick who had written to her 'was not the same one who married Oakley's daughter and to whom some suspicion attached of having some share in poor Tim

Hanley's murder'.[23] A direct consequence of the murder was that the extensive renovations of the castle were 'to be suspended until some person comes forward and make discovery as to the murder of her [Mrs Otway Cave's] servant'.[24]

A report on the state of County Tipperary written to the Chief Secretary William Lamb, in 1847, by a Major Powell gives some perception of the *mentalité* of rural communities. The people, he said, preferred to settle disputes by violence in preference to the arbitration of the law or interference of the resident gentry. Furthermore in relation to factions, he said,

> When any grievance arises to one of the party, it becomes a complaint of the whole body . . . and with the same alacrity will they come forward to assist in gathering harvest or any other service of kindness . . . neither chapel or funeral is held sacred and the fairs and markets have been destroyed by their proceedings.[25]

Powell added that the sons of farmers were all engaged in the faction combinations and were encouraged by their fathers and 'small occupiers of the land for the purpose of intimidating landlords from ejecting and bringing in new tenantry'.

Not all interpersonal disputes were resolved by resorting to violence, often tenants referred disputes to the landlord or agent for arbitration. The letters from tenants to the landlord indicate that for some this was the preferred solution to inter-personal conflict and the same sources give some insights into causes for tension between members of the community and indeed of families. A tenant from the Lissenhall estate petitioned Robert Otway Cave, because, as he stated, his father held a farm of twelve acres and gave 'my sister the Canny and mother six acres and so held until the last arrangement'. However, Wilson, the agent, was bribed and 'now I have only one acre and one perch' and am paying the Canny rent and have nothing'.[26]

In a period of increasing competition for land it is not difficult to see why disputes over land should predominate. The dwelling house of James Kennedy of Garryglass was attacked by men armed with stones and a gun, the motive being 'a farm of land of three acres formerly held by Ryans'.[27] Writing of the outrages in the neighbourhood of Borrisoleigh, James Ormsby reported that nearly thirty families were warned to leave adding that the armed men were 'calling persons settled there from twenty to thirty years strangers'.[28] The reason given for an attack on a filly, in Gorteenavalla in 1840, the property of Thomas Ryan of Ballintotty, was 'to intimidate persons from taking grass on the said townland, there being persons lately dispossessed out of the same by Otway Cave'.[29]

Some people were prepared to give information to the police, however, it is difficult to differentiate between those who assisted the police because of abhorrence at particular crimes and out of a sense of duty and those who were motivated by rewards and perhaps the chance to settle old scores. It was said that those who were not involved in outrages in the Borrisoleigh area in 1815 were unwilling to give information lest that information be given on 'their own illicit dealings in and with private distilleries, by which most of them exist'.[30] Following a riot at the fair at Castle Otway, Philip Kennedy gave 'valuable private information' to the constabulary and identified Michael Boland as the ring leader and a Michael Kennedy gave assistance to the police with the Hanley murder.[31]

References to sectarian tensions within the wider Templederry community are rare. Even taking cognizance of the overt bias of the *Tipperary Vindicator* which canvassed the support of 'Catholics and of all liberal Protestants in the neighbourhood', this newspaper carried some virulent accounts of celebrations marking the twelfth of July.[32] Shinrone, County Offaly, was, according to the *Tipperary Vindicator*, the scene of 'diabolical orgies' when in July 1844, Protestants,

> some half clad and armed to the teeth . . . poured in from Borrisokane, Cloughjordan and those favoured spots in the Ormonds which the Dutchman and hoary Cromwell planted with their fiery followers.[33]

Templederry was one of these favoured spots in the barony of Ormond, and it is quite possible that Protestants from Templederry attended these gatherings.

The Church of Ireland parish of Templederry was administered between 1783 and 1870 by a father and son succession, the Rev. Edward Jordan and the Rev. William Jordan. It would appear that Mr. William Jordan was a liberal Protestant which may have helped maintain good relations between the two religious communities on the estate. Relations between the spiritual leaders were sufficiently cordial for the pastor and priest to join in proposing a toast to the landlord R.J. Otway on his return from the Black Sea. Mr. Jordan who chaired the proceedings toasted the 'Catholic clergy and the health of Fr. Kenyon'.[34] A state-supported school system, under the National Board of Commissioners of National Education, which was set up in 1831, provided combined moral and literary instruction with separate doctrinal instruction.[35] Until 1897 Catholic and Protestant children were educated together in the national schools in Templederry. The first application for a grant for a Protestant school was made in that year by Rev. Samuel Armstrong.[36] This new school was named Castle Otway school. Whether this move towards separate national schools resulted from local demand or was motivated by Mr. Armstrong's own religious convictions remains to be seen. He published a pamphlet, in 1910, entitled *The Cooneyites or Dippers, a plain refutation of their errors.*[37] It was noted in the Templederry vestry book that several of the community, Joseph Shouldice and William Stanley, had gone over to the 'Cooneyites' in 1907 while Mr. Armstrong was rector in Templederry.[38]

The first national school in Templederry was built on land provided by Henry Hunt of Huntsgrove in the townland of Gortnagoona in 1844 and by 1850 a total of eighty pupils were registered as attending Templederry national school, the official name of the school. The application for assistance to the board of national education said that the 'district was wild and secluded and disturbed and there was no effective moral control on the youth'.[39] While the process of the institutionalisation of education and the proliferation of schools was under way in the greater Templederry area, nevertheless, in the pre-Famine era the formal education establishments constituted only a small part of a total education process. Of far more importance for socialization were the church, the community and above all the family, especially in transmitting cultural values.

The impact of organised religion in Templederry will be discussed here from the perspective of the majority religious group, the Catholic church. The keeping of parish registers by the Catholic clergy is seen as a key point in Tridentine Catholic organisation. The existence of registers can be used to measure the transition of the church from a local to a universal church, from a church with an oral perspective to one with a literate perspective and from a traditional to a modern world view.[40] The earliest entries in the Templederry Catholic registers are dated 1839.

The influence of the official church was diluted, at a time when it was emerging from the restrictions imposed upon it by the penal laws, by the relatively low levels of attendance at church services in the pre-Famine era. In 1835 the Catholic population of the combined civil parishes of Templederry and Latteragh was given as 2,691, with a further 2,077 in the parish of Killaneafe. The average attendance at Sunday Mass in 1835 was stated to be 850 in Templederry and 300–350 in Curreeny while about 600 people attended mass in Killaneafe which was served by the clergy from Templederry.[41] Allowing for those who would have been discharged from the obligation of hearing mass either through age or infirmity, these figures give a 35 per cent attendance at chapel on Sundays. It has been suggested that there is a discrepancy in the attendance figures as given in the report on public instruction in 1835. However, the Catholic clergy making the returns for the parishes of Templederry and Latteragh commented that the numbers attending at mass were increasing.[42] From this it can also be deduced that there was a concomitant rise in the profile of the priest and of his control and leadership within the community.

The newspapers of the period record some of the activities of the clergy as agents of moral and social reform. One area where they were active in modifying behaviour was in the temperance movement. Bands led 10,000 people, decorated with medals and shamrocks, according to the *Nenagh Gazette*, in a temperance march to Tyone in Nenagh, in 1841. There they were addressed by Rev. John Kenyon, curate in the parish of Silvermines, who admonished the crowd for 'irregularity and dissipation'.[43] Fr. Theobold

Mathew, the priest who was synonymous with the temperance movement, addressed a gathering in Templederry in 1845 but due to inclement weather the attendance was disappointing. [44]

However there were certain factors peculiar to the Catholic parish of Templederry, which militated against this general trend towards consolidation of spiritual life within the formal structures of the parish system and by extension limited the authority of the priest both in spiritual and temporal matters. One explanation for a diminished leadership role would be the character and extra-curricular activities of the priest Fr. John Kenyon, known as the 'Young Ireland priest'.[45] The most charitable assessment which could be made of the personality of Fr. Kenyon was that which was made by Mrs. Otway Cave when she wrote that 'a mind like Kenyon's . . . seems remarkably eccentric and variable'. [46]

Upon the retirement of the parish priest of Templederry in December 1842 Fr. Henry Carey was appointed administrator of Templederry and Fr. Kenyon was transferred from the neighbouring neighbouring parish of Silvermines to Templederry as curate. A dispute arose between Fr. Carey and Fr. Kenyon which went to an ecclesiastical trial in November 1847. The outcome was that the parish was divided with Fr. Carey as administrator in Killeen and Fr. Kenyon in Templederry. Kenyon's involvement with Young Ireland led to his suspension by the bishop of Killaloe, from 2 May to 14 June 1848, during which period Fr. Joseph McGrath was appointed administrator to Templederry. Fr. McGrath found the doors of the chapel at Templederry nailed and closed against him. Five or six parishioners who were there refused to let him enter the church. Instead he went to the chapel at Killeen and some of the respectable people of Templederry attended mass there. It was not until 1850 that Fr. Kenyon was appointed administrator over the whole parish and parish priest in 1860 following the death of Fr. Kennedy the parish priest.[47]

Fr. Kenyon was not only 'something of a problem to his brother priests', he could be equally quarrelsome in his relationships with secular members of the community.[48] Fr. Kenyon referred to a man named Kennedy, who had expressed an interest in providing postal services for the area, as a 'slovenly meecher'. Writing to the estate agent Fr. Kenyon said that he had heard that the aforementioned Kennedy had said that he, Kenyon, would be the last person he 'would sell the land to as I had never shewn [sic] him any countenance'.[49] A public dispute in which Fr. Kenyon was involved with the magistrates over an unauthorised building of a wall which encroached on the public highway was reported in the local paper. Fr. Kenyon was often absent from the parish, whether it was in connection with Young Ireland meetings in Dublin or visiting friends in County Down or Paris, where he baptised the daughter of John Mitchel in 1860.[50]

The sources for investigating local popular politics are scarce. While the estate records show that in 1778 Cooke Otway ordered '23 pairs of gayters and buttons' for the Castle Otway Volunteers, from Charles Murphy, 'gaytermaker', no further information has come to light as to the size or membership on the volunteer corps.[51] The Castle Otway corps was not listed in the 1784 return of volunteers of Ireland but it is conceivable that it was subsumed into either the Ormond Independents under Colonel Toler or the Ormond Union commanded by Colonel Prittie, as both of these men were related to Cooke Otway.[52] The only information on the rebellion of 1798 in the greater Nenagh area is derived from Musgrave's *Memoirs of the different rebellions in Ireland*, an account which is written from a loyalist perspective.[53] Mr. Cooke Otway, it was asserted, had proof that the people in 'his populous parish were sworn, organised and well supplied with arms'. Furthermore Cooke Otway was 'the most active person in the County of Tipperary, next to Colonel Fitzgerald, in putting down rebellion'. He was forced to disband the Catholic members of his yeomanry corps' as they had taken the United Irishmen's oath'.[54]

From the 1760s to the 1840s, popular protest was an almost constant feature of Irish society. The underlying causes of this unrest appear to be much more complex than that presented by the poor Catholic peasant in opposition to the rackrenting English Protestant landlord scenario or the alternate farmer versus labourers stereotype.[55] Yet, the records of central government do not note any specific incidents in the Castle Otway area associated with the main agrarian movements of the period such as Whiteboyism or Rightboys or the Tithe campaign of the 1830s. An analyses of Whiteboy activity in Tipperary in the period 1760–80 records four outbreaks near Nenagh and a couple of incidents near Borrisoleigh.[56]

The records which have survived often present conflicting views on the state of the county. It is difficult to reconcile the description of Mr. Going, of Traveston, Silvermines, of a county 'in a perfect state of tranquillity' showing 'no disposition existing among them tending to anything bordering on rebellion' with that of neighbouring Borrisoleigh as 'the centre of a disturbed district' and that there was a need for more troops.[57] This last request was made by George Ryan of Inch House, a Catholic landlord, outside Borrisoleigh on the 7 June 1815 while Going's letter was dated 16 June 1815.

At a meeting of magistrates held in Nenagh in May 1815 a reward of £100 was offered for the conviction of persons who were posting threatening notices. Henry Otway attended this meeting and subscribed £50 to establish a committee to represent the magistrates. Arthur Carden, of Barnane, Templemore, a commander in the militia, following a search for arms which included the Castle Otway area, wrote that 'it would be a crying shame not to proclaim Templederry and Kilfitmor . . . as they contain a concentration of mischief in themselves.'[58] While 'this place is going head to the Devil' it would be naive to imagine that Templederry remained isolated from these events.[59] Ten years later in May 1825 Upper Ormond was one of the baronies proclaimed under the Insurrection Act, later revoked in June 1825.[60]

Some of the official correspondence relating to the political activities of Fr. Kenyon in Templederry in the period prior to the uprising of 1848 are missing. However, it was recorded that the sub-inspector for the Borrisoleigh district submitted reports on Fr. Kenyon, on a meeting to elect delegates for a National Council and also on recruiting for Young Ireland in Garryglass in May 1848.[61]

A contrasting view of popular politics is provided by the local newspapers. In June 1844 a meeting was held in Templederry to protest at the imprisonment of Daniel O'Connell which Maurice Lenihan, editor of the *Tipperary Vindicator*, attended at the invitation of some of the priests. John Dwyer Ryan of Castle Otway proposed a boycott or 'non-intercourse with non Repealers' which was seconded by William Boland of Boulabane. A sum of £32 was collected for the repeal fund and apart from one or two of the contributors who can be identified it is not possible to deduce from the list of subscribers how strong was the Castle Otway community representation at the meeting. John Hunt of Huntsgrove gave £2.4s.6d. and John Dwyer Ryan gave £5.10s.0d.

Who exactly John Dwyer Ryan was is unclear. Some of speakers can be identified but they were from the wider parish of Templederry and not from the estate community, J.P. Kennedy from Ballyhane, William O'Leary from Cooneen and William Boland from Boulabane. While the gathering was described as 'a numerous and highly respectable meeting at the parish church' this statement should not be taken as an indication of widespread interest or involvement in popular politics, as the attendance included Richard Cooke of Rathmoy, Borrisoleigh, T. Fitzpatrick, a solicitor from Nenagh and Fr. Meagher, parish priest of Toomevara, all from outside the area.[62] It was noted in the newspaper that 'several cars went out from Nenagh, Borrisoleigh and the neighbouring towns and villages'. Many, it seemed 'took advantage to visit the romantic scenery of castle Otway and Templederry'.[63] The fact that so many people who attended were from outside the parish raises the question as to whether the whole meeting was orchestrated to counteract the influence of Fr. John Kenyon and Young Ireland.

James Fintan Lalor visited Templederry in October 1847 and massgoers were urged by Fr. Kenyon to follow him to Menough church to form a tenant league. The *Tipperary Vindicator* claimed that 'very few, few indeed followed the gentleman's advice'.[64] Lalor 'commenced long and loud harangues to address the most excitable people in Tipperary. The most respectable farmers turned away with disgust and returned to their homes'. Fr. Kenyon's opposition to Daniel O'Connell was widely covered in the *Tipperary Vindicator* and Maurice Lenihan, the editor of the *Vindicator*, was equally vehement in his antagonism to the priest. Kenyon's antipathy to O'Connell extended to 'ridiculing and insulting O'Connell's funeral'.[65] This stance of Kenyon must have divided the community which was already polarised, according to a report on the Tenant League meeting, on socio-economic lines.

It would appear from the newspaper accounts that the leadership in local political activity, apart from Fr. Kenyon, came largely from outside the Castle Otway community. The impetus for the establishment of national schools in the parish of Templederry also came from outside the estate. William O'Leary from Cooneen who was one of those named as attending the Repeal meeting in Templederry was also one of the trustees for the schools in Gortnagoona and in Latteragh.[66] Some of those named in the newspaper reports of Repeal meetings held in Templederry; Hunt of Gortnagoona and Kennedy of Ballyhane, also represented the wider Templederry community at county level. J.P. Kennedy was a member of the board of guardians of the Nenagh poor law union and he was one of the first Catholics from Templederry whose participation in local government can be traced. John Hunt and John Kennedy attended a meeting in Nenagh to select a member of parliament for the county following the death of the sitting MP, Robert Otway Cave.[67] In November 1845 at a board of guardians' meeting in Nenagh Kennedy presented a petition for the repeal of the act of union.[68]

The reticence of the folk memory of the Great Famine, in an ironic way, articulates the impact of this catastrophe on the community.

> The famine of 1846 did not affect this district very much. There is no account of any people dying round here except one poor scholar whose name is unknown was found dead near Kilcommon ... He came from the Doon [County Limerick] side and was nearly dead from hunger when he arrived here.[69]

From this account there is a sense of 'othering of the victim', the victim is a stranger. Other accounts emphasise death through disease,

> they had to eat grass and blackberries and crabs and on that account they got the plague. The cholera came and took the people away in great numbers.[70]

perhaps because of a stigma associated with death through starvation. This pithy account of the catastrophe, distancing as it does the survivors from the disaster conveys a greater sense of the trauma experienced by the community than does any demographic study.

The population of the combined civil parishes of Templederry and Latteragh declined by 30 per cent between 1841 and 1851, however the population loss on the Otway estate was slightly lower at 27 per cent. These figures obscure the fact that the population loss was not uniform in the different townlands, either in the estate or in the combined parishes, indeed a couple of townlands showed a slight increase in population in 1851. The population in Gortnagoona, for example, fell by 61 per cent from 255 to 99 people, in Cloghonan it was

37 per cent. In some of the marginal townlands the loss was not as significant, the Rusheen More population decreased by 2 per cent and in Rusheen Beg it was 13 per cent and in Garryglass the decline was 21 per cent. Some townlands experienced a gain in population, the population in Curreeny increased by 5 per cent, in Shanballyard 3 per cent. According to the census of 1841, there was nobody living in the townland of Killavalla, by 1851 there were eleven people living there.

This quantitative evidence on changes in population does not distinguish between demographic changes which were already in place prior to 1845, between deaths due to starvation and or disease or population loss due to emigration, nor can the different experiences of the social classes be compared. Does the evidence suggest that farmers in the higher value townlands, such as Templederry, which lost 40 per cent of its population, as opposed to Glanaguile where the population decreased by 74 per cent, were in a position to emigrate? The rise in the population in some of the lower value townlands suggests a certain degree of relocation of displaced persons to these marginal area.

From the official records we can observe how the community responded to the disaster facing it. A relief committee was established in the Templederry and Latteragh area with members drawn from local clergy, landlords and farmers. The Frs Kenyon, Carey and Jordan were members as were landlords Caleb Going and John Hunt and representing farmers were James Ryan, John Ardell, Philip Cantwell and William Coughlan. The latter was probably the miller in Garrane. The three clergymen also served on the relief committee in Dolla and Killaneave.[71]

Writing about the conditions in Templederry, in April 1846, Kenyon said that the potato supply was nearly exhausted and that the people were eating the seed potatoes and he added that they were being charged an 'exorbitant price for Indian meal'.[72] In May of the same year he stressed the urgent need for the opening of the public works sanctioned at Greenane, 'before fever appears amongst its starving population otherwise it may be too late'. He also acknowledged receipt of a £60 donation from the lord lieutenant. Several days later he again wrote and said that he had seen 'several persons who had eaten but four potatoes up to a late hour in the evening'. In Templederry, he said, half the crop had been lost and half of the labourers were idle.[73] Fr. Morris, parish priest of Borrisoleigh, also emphasised the plight of the labourers when he described how '150 labourers marched into this town' demanding work, he said that a quarter of the labourers were in need of employment.[74]

A subscription list was sent to the relief committee to support the request for grants to match local contributions. Mrs. Otway Cave topped the list with a subscription of £30, Lord Dunalley gave £10, Kenyon himself contributed £17, Jordan £4, and the rector from Latteragh Mr. Studdert £2. The remainder of the local fund of £100 was made up of the donations from the farmers, the majority of whom can be identified as Castle Otway tenants;

George Powell, William Mooney, Mrs. Guilmartin, Simon Young, William Boland, John Hodgins, all of whom gave 10s. John Ardell and Thomas Dagg contributed £1 each and Peter Tucker 5s.[75] Mrs. Otway Cave also headed the Borrisoleigh Poor Relief Fund contributing £30.[76] Kenyon noted most vigorously in his letters to the relief committee that Lord Orkney, the major landlord in Latteragh had ignored all requests for contributions.

The records of central government tend to weigh the balance quite conspicuously on the side of conflict and the failure of community relations. By reverse inference, it is also feasible to use the same records to reconstruct the norms which the community at large particularly wished to protect. The correspondence between the local relief committee and central relief agency presents a more affirmative representation of a community putting aside religious, political, class and personal differences and disagreements to work together in the face of the calamity of the potato failure.

Conclusion

This pamphlet presents a new understanding of the relationship between the landlords of the Otway estate and their tenants, one which challenges the general stereotype of rack renting evicting landlords. In particular it is argued that Thomas Otway has been unfairly judged in the past. In taking a proactive approach to the management of his property which was sometimes reflected in an unsentimental approach to the violations of estate rules, he has been condemned as a 'petty tyrant'.[1] Indeed a causal link has been suggested between the role of the Otways as 'stern landlords' and the burning of the castle on the estate in 1921.[2]

The examination of the early nineteenth-century financial records does not support the view of a tenantry subjected to arbitrary increases in rents or of the bulk of the tenantry insecure in their holdings. While there is evidence that some tenants were given notices to quit and that the formalities necessary for an eviction to have legal standing were observed on the estate, it has not been possible to assess the scale of evictions on the Otway estate. Economic interdependence was woven through the fabric of the lives of the tenants and the landlord and the economic life of the community was marked by the fluctuations in market conditions. This micro-economy was highly sensitive to the vicissitudes of the market economy and this factor had as much impact on the sustainability of Otway estate community as had any actions on the part of the landlord.

In using the particular relationship between the landlord and the tenant as the focal point of the investigation something of the dynamics of the internal world of this community, the Castle Otway estate community, has been revealed. It is no longer appropriate to categorise this community as a group of people undifferentiated in their resources to maintain themselves and their families. The evidence from the leases and rent rolls portrays a community which had evolved from one in which the cottier had lost his numerically pre-eminent position to one dominated by the tenant farmer with larger farms concentrated in the higher value townlands. The preferred settlement in the poorer townlands was for smaller holdings and nucleated settlement.

By the 1850s the landlord was no longer the principal channel of communication between Castle Otway and the outside world. He was no longer the sole broker articulating and transferring information, ideas and opinions up and down the social ladder. The community's horizons were also being pushed back through its links with the wider world; through newspapers, emigration, more contact with central government through the new agencies for welfare and education and social control. His dominant position in local affairs was being suc-cessfully challenged with representatives now coming from within the community.

This is by no means the complete story of this estate community's expe-rience. The estate records only deal with those who had official contacts with the landlord. The experiences of labourers can only be generalised about from external sources. By and large official records deal with those people who came into conflict with the law or those who were marginalized by their utter destitution. The particular incidents detailed in the crime reports do not provide a long range view of social tensions but more of a specific view of tension and pressure indigenous to this given area. The records of central government tend to weigh the balance conspicuously on the side of conflict and the failure of community relationships.

The quantitative analyses of the rent rolls in some ways sanitises the realities of the poverty of life in Templederry. One of those realities not brought out by the estate records is the fact that the vast majority of people lived in sub-standard housing. Out of a total of 301 houses in the civil parish of Templederry in 1851, 259 were third and fourth class houses, fourth class houses were one roomed cabins and third class were cottages, mud cottages with two to four rooms and with windows.[3] The impact of the economic crisis of 1815 following the loss of valuable overseas markets has been analysed. What were the con-sequences of the subsistence crisis of 1755, 1766, 1783, 1800–1, 1816–19 on the community, of the wet and cold summers of 1822 and 1830 and of the typhus epidemic of 1819?[4] There is a gamut of human experiences and emotions, both at personal level and community level, which remain hidden for ever.

The Castle Otway community has been observed going through a period of change which effected both landlords and tenants. While change is discernible over the period 1750–1853, there were nevertheless elements of stability and continuity. The core families who farmed on the estate as tenants over the period of study, Ryan 'Counsellor', Ryans of Oatfield, Hodgins of Garryglass, Powells of the Felix would have played a role in providing the community with stability and identity.

It is appropriate that the final commentary on the wider topic of landlord tenant relations and in particular of the Otway family as landlords should be left to the community itself. The differing perspectives are in themselves indicitative of the complexity of that relationship. Lord Dunalley, one of the landlords in Curreeny was 'considered good by some tenants and very bad by others'.[5] In contrast

The Otways were always looked upon as good landlords.
They gathered no tithes from the people . . .
Otway's ancestors were captains in Cromwell's army in 1649.
There were no people evicted in this district.[6]

Appendix

OTWAY FAMILY TREE 1750–1853

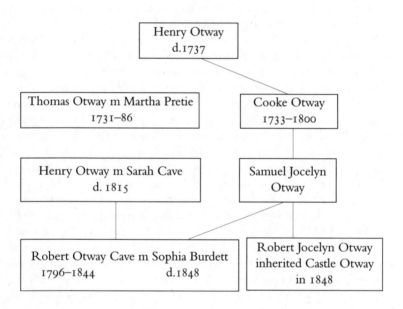

Source: Burke's landed gentry of Ireland. 4th ed. London 1958.

Notes

ABBREVIATIONS

CG   *Clonmel Gazette*
CSORP   Chief Secretary's Office, Registered Papers
LCA   Leicester City Archives
NA   National Archives
NG   *Nenagh Guardian*
NLI   National Library of Ireland
OP   Outrage Papers
SOC   State of the Country Papers
TCL   Tipperary County Library
TV   *Tipperary Vindicator*

INTRODUCTION

1 *CG*, 7–10 Jan 1778.
2 NA, LEC 25/20: Rental of the several townlands situated in the baronies of Upper Ormond and Kilnamanagh, and in the County of Tipperary, the estate of the said Robert Otway, esq, which will be sold for auction by the Commissioners for sale of in cumbered estates in Ireland, Thursday, the 1st day of December, 1853.
3 Thomas U. Sadleir, 'Manuscripts at Kilboy, County Tipperary, in the possession of Lord Dunalley' in *Analecta Hibernica* no. 12 (1943), pp 113–54.
4 W.E. Vaughan, *Landlords and tenants in mid-Victorian Ireland* (Oxford, 1994).
5 R.D. Crotty, *Irish agricultural production, the historical background* (Chicago, 1975), p. 20.
6 *Dublin Evening Post*, 22 Sept 1853.
7 *TV*, 31 Jan. 1844, 12 June 1844.
8 *TV*, 30 March 1844.
9 William Nolan (ed), *Tipperary: history and society* (Dublin, 1985).
10 W.J. Smyth, 'Estate records and the making of the Irish landscape: an example from County Tipperary' in *Ir. Geography, ix* (1976), pp 29–49.
11 Thomas Power, *Land, politics and society in eighteenth century Tipperary* (Oxford, 1993); Donal Murphy, *The two Tipperarys* (Nenagh, 1994).
12 Evidence of William Henry Head to the Devon commission 1844, *Devon comm. rep.* H.C. 1845 [605], xix, 1–56, p. 636.

THE LANDLORD

1 NLI, MS 8147: Peerage of Tipperary.
2 R.C. Simington, (ed.), *The civil survey ad. 1654–56* (10 vols., Dublin, 1931–36), ii, pp 214–31.
3 Seamus Pender, (ed.), *Census of Ireland circa 1659, with supplementary material from the poll money ordnance 1660–1* (Dublin, 1939), p. 322.
4 *The civil survey*, ii, p. 230.

5 Letters patent for granting a free and general pardon to Ltd. John Otway, petition presented by earl of Mountrath, dated 21 Jan. 1661 in *Calendar of state papers, Ireland, Charles II 1660–62* (London, 1905), p. 158. William Smyth, 'Property, patronage and population, reconstructing the human geography of seventeenth-century county Tipperary ' in William Nolan (ed.), *Tipperary, history and society* (Dublin, 1985), pp 104–138.

6 LCA, 23D 57/739: Bargain and sale between John Stafford of Sligo, yeoman and John Otway of Sligo, 7 Aug 1660.

7 J.G. Simms, 'Cromwellian settlement of Tipperary' in *Tipperary Historical Journal*, 1989, pp 27–32.

8 *Census of Ireland circa* 1659, p. 320.

9 Bruce Elliott, *Irish migrants in the Canadas: a new approach* (Belfast, 1988), p. 15.

10 *Clonmel Gazette* April 3–7 1788.

11 NLI, MS 11416: An account of the tenants of Anthony Parker esq. in County Tipperary and County Limerick 1784.

12 NLI, MS 352: Abstract of information in answer to queries concerning the parishes in the diocese of Killaloe and Kilfenora 1820; Thomas Power, *Land, politics and society in eighteenth-century Tipperary* (Oxford, 1993), pp 18–9.

13 NLI, MS 13000(8): Otway estate papers, seven nineteenth century rent rolls 1801–1825 (hereafter cited as rent rolls): interview with Freda Powell, The Felix, Templederry. County Tipperary, Oct. 1996.

14 *Second report of the commissioners of Irish education inquiry*, H.C. 1826–27 (2), xii, 1, pp 1152–3, pp 1132–5.

15 *First report of the commissioners of public instruction Ireland*, H.C. 1835 (45), (46), xxxiii, 1.

16 *Burke's landed gentry of Ireland*, 4th ed. (London, 1958), pp 616–18.

17 NA, MS 3396: Certified entries in parish records.

18 *Index to prerogative wills of Ireland 1536–1810*, ed. Sir Arthur Vicars (Dublin, 1897), p. 363.

19 Maurice Craig, *Classic Irish houses of the middle size* (London, 1976), p. 122.

20 *The civil survey*, p. 230.

21 *Letters containing information relative to the antiquities of the county of Tipperary collected during the progress of the Ordnance Survey 1840*, ed. Michael Flanagan (Bray, 1930), p. 190.

22 NLI, MS 12138: Ledger of accounts 1771–72. Michael Hewson, 'Eighteenth century directions to servants in County Tipperary' in Etienne Rynne (ed.), *North Munster studies, essays in commemoration of Monsignor Michael Moloney* (Limerick, 1967), pp 332–4. A spalpeen was an itinerant farm labourer, *Webster's Third International Dictionary* (London, 1981).

23 NLI, MS 12138: Ledger of accounts 1771–72.

24 NLI, MS 12139: Ledger of accounts 1778–79.

25 NLI, MS 12139: Ledger of accounts 1778–79.

26 S.J. Connolly, *Priest and people in Pre-famine Ireland* (Dublin, 1982), p. 169.

27 Michael Hewson, 'Eighteenth century directions to servants in County Tipperary' in Rynne (ed.), *North Munster studies*, p. 334.

28 NA, CSORP OP papers: 1838 TY 27/521

29 NLI, MS 12138: Ledger of accounts 1771–72. Seacole or sea kale is a root crop grown for fodder, *Webster's Third International Dictionary* (London, 1981).

30 *Proceedings of the Dublin Society*, iii (1766–1767), pp 492–3.

31 NLI, MS 12138: Ledger of accounts 1771–72.

32 NLI, MS 12141: Thomas Ryder
    Pepper's accounts with the tenants
    1816–23.
33 NLI, MS 12142: Ledger of accounts
    1845.
34 NLI, MS 12139: Ledger of accounts
    1778–79.
35 LCA, 23D57/977: Lease between
    Thomas Otway and Charles
    MacDaniel 13 Feb 1773.
36 Conversation with John Kennedy,
    Shanballyard, Templederry,
    Co. Tipperary, Oct. 1996.
37 LCA, MS 23D57/977: Lease for
    lives between Thomas Otway and
    Charles MacDaniel.
38 Conrad Gill, *The rise of the linen
    industry* (Oxford, 1925), pp 122–8.
39 NA, Tipp. 5.1821: Primary Valuation,
    Parish of Latteragh, House books.
40 NLI, MS 12139: Ledger of accounts
    1778–79.
41 TV 14 Dec 1844.
42 NLI, MS 17,712: Irish national land
    league memorandum as to the cases
    of rack-renting, signed by Patrick
    Glynn C.C., Killeen House,
    Templederry, Co. Tipperary.
43 NLI, MS 13536: Letter from Cooke
    Otway to Cooper Crawford 30 Nov
    1789.
44 NA, MS 3391: A bill for vesting
    certain parts of the real estates devised
    by the will of Thomas Otway, 43
    Geo. III 1803, 'not proceeded with'
    was written on the manuscript.
45 *Templederry, my home: a parish history*
    (Templederry, 1980), p. 49.
46 Jack Simmons, *Leicester past and
    present , ancient borough to 1860*,
    (2 vols., London, 1974), i, p. 146.
47 TV 11 Feb 1844.
48 TV 7 Dec 1844.
49 NLI, MS 13004(4): Letter from Mrs.
    Otway Cave to Edwin Taylor 10
    Nov 1848.
50 NLI, MS 13004(4): Letter from Mrs.
    Otway Cave to Edwin Taylor 19
    Dec 1848.
51 NLI, MS 13004 (4): Letter from
    Mrs. Otway Cave to William
    Stephens 5 May 1847.
52 NLI, MS 13004(4): Letter from Rev.
    John Kenyon to Mrs. Otway Cave
    [undated].
53 NLI, MS 13004(4): Letter from Mrs.
    Otway Cave to William Stephens 25
    May 1847.
54 NLI, MS13004(3): Letter from Mrs.
    Otway Cave to E. Taylor 30 Jan 1848.
55 NLI, MS13004(3): Letter from Mrs.
    Otway Cave to E. Taylor 30 Jan 1848.
56 NLI, MS 13004(4): Rent roll 1814.
57 NLI, MS 13536: Letter from Rev.
    S.J. Otway to Robert Otway Cave,
    30 April 1827.
58 NLI, MS 13004(4): Letter from Mrs.
    Otway Cave to William Stephens,
    10 Nov 1847.
59 NLI, MS 13004(4): Letter from
    William Carr to Robert Otway
    Cave, 28 May 1827.
60 TV 15 June 1844.
61 Donal Murphy, *The two Tipperarys*
    (Nenagh, 1994), p. 48, p. 59.
62 NLI, MS 13536: Letter from Cooke
    Otway to Cooper Crawford, 15
    June 1788.
63 Bruce Elliott, *Irish migrants in the
    Canadas: a new approach* (Belfast,
    1988).
64 NLI, MS 12138: Ledger of accounts
    1771–2.
65 NLI, MS 13000(8): Rent rolls
    1801–1825.
66 LCA, 23D52/1030: Rent roll 1811.
67 NLI, 13004(3): Rent roll 1823.

THE TENANTRY

1   Arthur Young, *A tour in Ireland ... in
    the years 1776, 1777 and 1778.* ed.
    Constantia Maxwell (Cambridge,
    1925); *First report from the commissioners
    for inquiring into the conditions of the
    labouring poor, appendix (A,) and
    supplement,* H.C. 1835 (369), xxxii, pt

_oor Inquiry (Ireland). Appendix (D),
containing baronial examinations relative
to earnings of labourers, cottier tenants,
employ of children and expenditure and
supplement containing answers to questions
1 to 12 circulated by the commissioners,
H.C. 1836 [36], xxxi, pt 1; Poor inquiry,
(Ireland) Appendix E baronial examinations relative to food, cottages and savings
banks, drinking with supplement containing answers to questions, H.C. 1836
[37], xxxii, pt 1; Report from her
majesty's commissioners of inquiry into
the state of the law and practice in
respect to the occupation of land in
Ireland, H.C. 1845, [605], xix.

2 NLI, MS 12139: Ledger 1778–9.
3 NLI, MS 12140: Ledger 1780–81.
4 NLI, MS 12139: Ledger 1778–9.
'Counsellor' was and is a nickname
used to distinguish me of the
numerous Ryan families.
5 NLI, MS 12139: Ledger 1778–9.
6 NLI, MS 12139: Ledger 1778–9.
7 NA, CSORP OP Tipperary 1838
TY27/521:18 Sept 1838.
8 NLI, MS 13000(4): Rent rolls 1806–
1825.
9 NLI, MS 12138: Ledger 1777–1778.
10 W.E.Vaughan, Landlords and tenants in
mid-Victorian Ireland. (Oxford, 1994).
W.A. Maguire, The Downshire estates
in Ireland 1801–45, the management of
Irish landed estates in the nineteenth-
century. (Oxford,1972), p. 1.
11 Maureen Wall 'The age of the penal
laws (1691–1778)' in T.W. Moody
and F.X. Martin (eds) The course of
Irish History (Cork, 1987), pp 217–231.
12 Thomas Power, Land, politics and
society in eighteenth-century Tipperary
(Oxford, 1993).
13 T.W. Freeman, Pre-famine Ireland, a
study in historical geography (Manchester,
1957), p. 15.
14 W. H. Crawford, Aspects of Irish social
history 1750–1800 (Belfast, 1969), p. 3.
15 NLI, MS 13003: Letter from Rev.
Richard Lloyd to Robert Otway
Cave 26 March 1828.

16 Maguire, The Downshire estates;
Crawford, Aspects of Irish social
history, p. 3.
17 Power Land, politics, pp 113–4.
18 John Lanigan was identified by the
Tipperary Vindicator as a Catholic, TV,
30 Mar 1844.
19 NA, LEC 25/20: Rental of the several
townlands ...
20 Devon Comm. report, Appendix B, p.
31.
21 NA, D 20364: Lease between Thomas
Otway and James Otway 1752.
22 NA, D 20367: Deed between Thomas
Otway and John Lloyd, 24 May 1758.
23 CG, 6 April 1789.
24 CG, 21 November 1789.
25 NLI, MS 13003: Letter from Rev.
Richard Lloyd to Robert Otway
Cave 26 March 1828.
26 TV, 24 Nov 1847.
27 TV, 24 Nov 1847.
28 TV, 29 Dec 1847.
29 NA, D 20371, D 20372: Leases
between Thomas Otway and James
Lee, 7 Jan 1761.
30 Thomas U. Sadleir, 'Manuscripts at
Kilboy, County Tipperary, in the possession of Lord Dunalley' in Analecta
Hibernica, no.12 (1943), pp 113–154.
31 NLI, GO MS 442: List of freeholders
of County Tipperary 1776.
32 Forty shilling freeholder was an occupier owning or renting land valued at
40s. or more, leaseholds for lives were
deeded to be freeholds,T.W. Freeman,
Pre-famine Ireland, p. 15.
33 TV, 14 Feb 1844.
34 R.V. Comerford, 'Tipperary representation at Westminster 1801–1918', in
William Nolan (ed.), Tipperary, history
and society (Dublin, 1985), pp 325.
35 LCA. 23D57/983: Lease between
Cooke Otway and William Welch,
Michael Welch, Michael Kennedy
and Patrick Kennedy 30 May 1787.
36 NA, D 20376: Lease between Thomas
Otway and Tim, Martin and John
Ryan, 1772.

37 NLI, MS 13004(3): Rent roll 1823.

38 NLI, MS 12138: Ledger 1772.

39 NLI, MS 12138: Ledger 1772.

40 NLI, MS 12138: Ledger 1772.

41 LCA, 23D57/975; Lease between Thomas Otway and John Ryan 13 Jan 1773; LCA, 23 D57/976: Lease between Thomas Otway and John Ryan 30 Jan 1773.

42 LCA, 23D57/ 979: Lease between Thomas Otway and John Ryan 24 June 1776.

43 LCA, 23D57/981: Lease between John Ryan and Patrick McLoughney 27 Oct 1776.

44 NLI, MS 17,712 Report to the Land League from Fr. Glynn, curate Killeen, Templederry, County Tipperary, 1870.

45 NLI, MS 21.f.15 Map of Garryglass 1772.

46 NLI, MS 12139: Ledger 1778–9.

47 NLI, MS 21.f.15: Map of Garryglass 1772; Kevin Whelan 'An underground gentry: Catholic middlemen in eighteenth-century Ireland' in *Eighteenth-century Ireland*, x (1995), pp 7–68.

48 NLI, MS 12,139: Ledger 1778–9, loose page p. 80.

49 NLI, MS 13000(4): Rent rolls 1806–1825.

50 NLI, MS 13000(4): Rent rolls 1806–1825.

51 LCA, 23D57/1020: Lease made between Julian Ryan and John McLoughney, Thomas McLoughney Sen., Thomas McLoughney Jun., and Edmond Mulcahy 26 Jan 1805.

52 LCA, 23D57/980: Lease John Ryan and Thomas Kennedy 8 Aug 1776; LCA, 23D57/981: Lease between John Ryan and Patrick McLoughney 27 Oct 1776.

53 Power, *Land, politics*, p. 142.

54 L. M. Cullen, 'Economic development 1750–1800', in W.E. Vaughan (ed.) *A new history of Ireland, vol. 5, Ireland under the Union, 1, 1801–70*, (Oxford, 1989), p. 174.

55 NLI, MS 21.f.15: Map of the Otway estate 1793.

56 NLI, MS 21.f.15: Map of the Otway estate 1793.

57 LCA, 23D57/1015: Lease between Henry Otway and Leonard Shouldice 11 May.

58 NLI, MS 13000(8): Rent roll 1806.

59 L.M. Cullen, *An economic history of Ireland since 1660* (London, 1972), p. 114.

60 *Economic history of Ireland since 1660*, p. 114. Power, *Land, politics*, p. 147.

61 NLI, MS 13003: Letter from Rev. Richard Lloyd to Robert Otway Cave 26 March 1828.

62 NA, D 20387: Mortgage deed 1834.

63 NA, LEC 25/20: *Rental of the several townlands*.

64 Power, *Land, politics*, pp 157–8; Crawford, *Aspects of Irish social history,* p. 3.

65 LCA, 23D57/997: Lease between Henry Otway and Thomas Lee 11 May 1801.

66 LCA, 23D/57 994: Lease between Henry Otway and Adam Hodgins 11 May 1801.

67 LCA, 23D57/1006: Lease between Henry Otway and Michael Oakley 11 May 1801.

68 NA, D.20365: Lease between Thomas Otway and John Short and Richard Branton 1752.

69 NLI, MS 15055(1): Letter from William and James Lee to Cooke Otway 11 Feb 1794.

70 NLI, MS. 13000(8): Rent rolls 1823, 1825.

71 NLI, MS. 13000(8): Rent roll 1825.

72 NLI, MS 12141: Ledger of accounts 1818.

73 NLI, MS 12141: Ledger of accounts 1818.

74 Freeman, *Pre-famine Ireland*, p.15; Cullen, *An economic history of Ireland since 1660*, pp 117–118.

75 In calculating the measure of central tendency in this research project the

median was used in preference to the mean because the wide range of farm sizes distorted the overall picture.

76 NA, D 20387: Deed of mortgage 1834.

77 NA, D 20387: Deed of mortgage 1834.

78 NLI, MS 13000(8): Rent roll 1819.

79 Michael Flanagan, (ed.) *Letters containing information relating to the antiquities of the County of Tipperary collected during the progress of the Ordnance Survey 1840*, (Bray, 1930) p. 215.

80 NA, Valuation Office Field Books Tipperary 4.3279: Field book of the primary valuation of the parish of Kilmore in the barony of Upper Ormond, County Tipperary, 1845.

81 Kevin Whelan , 'Pre and post famine landscape change' in Cathal Portéir (ed.) *The great Irish famine* (Dublin, 1995), pp 19–33.

82 Reminiscences of Fr. John Kennedy, Bourna, County Tipperary, transcript now in the possession of Marian Harrington, Cloghinch, Templederry, County Tipperary.

83 NA, Valuation Office Field Books Tipperary 4.4482: Field book of the primary valuation of the parish of Aghnameadle in the barony of Upper Ormond, County Tipperary, 1845.

84 NA, D20387: Deed of mortgage 1834.

85 NLI, MS 13000(8): Rent roll 1825.

86 NLI, MS 352: Abstract of information in answer to queries concerning the parishes of Killaloe and Kilfenora in 1820.

87 *First report from the commissioners for inquiring into the conditions of the labouring poor, appendix A, p. 31*, H.C. 1835 [369], xxxii.1.

88 *NG*, 27 March 1841.

89 NA, Valuation Office Field Books Tipperary 4.4482: Field book of the primary valuation of the townland of Ballyphillip in the parish of Kilmore in the barony of Upper Ormond, County Tipperary, 1845.

90 TCL, Poor law rate books for the union of Nenagh, parish of Templederry 1845–??.

91 Cormac Ó Gráda, 'Poverty, population, and agriculture, 1801–45' in W.E. Vaughan (ed.) *A new history of Ireland*, vol. 5, p. 108; Cullen, *An economic history of Ireland since 1660*, p. 103.

92 NLI, MS 13000(8): Rent rolls 1806–1825.

93 Maguire, *The Downshire estates in Ireland 1801–45*, pp 59–61.

94 NLI, MS 13000(8): Rent rolls 1806–1825.

THE COMMUNITY

1 Evelyn Lord, 'Communities of common interest: the social landscape of south-east Surrey, 1750– 1850', in Charles Phythian-Adams (ed.), *Societies, cultures and kinship, 1580–1850, cultural provinces and English local history*, (Leicester, 1993), p. 178.

2 The parish registers of the Catholic parish of Templederry begin in 1840 for baptisms and 1839 for marriages. The earliest surviving registers for the Church of Ireland registers are dated 1845.

3 NLI, MS13000(8): Rent rolls 1813, 1825; NA, D 20386: Mortgage deed 1827.

4 NLI, MS12139: Ledger 1778; NLI, MS 12140: Ledger 1780–1; NLI, MS 12141: Ledger 1818–1824.

5 NLI, MS 12140: Ledger 1780–1; LCA, 23D57/1020: Lease between Julian Ryan and John Mullanghny and others 26 Jan 1805.

6 NLI, MS 12139: Ledger 1778.

7 Dermot Gleeson, 'A day in Upper Ormond' in *Molua*, 1953, pp 19–26, p. 23.

8 *First report from the commissioners for inquiring into the condition of the poor in Ireland,with appendix (A.) and supplement*, H.C. 1835 (369), xxxii, pt. 1 p. 260.

9 Meitheal, 'working party' in Niall Ó Donaill (ed), *Foclóir Gaeilge-Béarla* (Dublin, 1977), p. 853; Timothy O'Neill, *Life and tradition in rural Ireland*, (London, 1977), p. 89.

10 NLI, MS 12142: Account book 1845.

11 Evidence of James Jocelyn Poe to the Devon commission, *Report from her majesty's commissioners of inquiry into the state of the law and practice in respect to the occupation of land in Ireland* [earl of Devon, chairman], H.C., 1845 [605], xix, 1–56, p. 639.

12 Cuaird= circuit, cuairt = visit; Kevin Whelan, 'The bases of region-alism' in Proinsias Ó Drisceoil (ed.), *Culture in Ireland – regions: identity and power* (Belfast,1993), p. 5–62.

13 *TV*, 17 Feb 1844.

14 NA, CSORP OP: TY1838, 27/440.

15 NA, CSORP OP: TY 1838, 27/521.

16 NA, CSORP OP: TY1838, 27/471.

17 NA, CRF Transportation records: 1836 c 43.

18 NLI, MS 13004(4): Letter from Mrs. Otway Cave to William Stephens 10 Nov 1848.

19 *TV*, 13 Oct 1847.

20 *NG*, 9 Oct 1847.

21 *TV*, 13 Oct 1847.

22 NA, D20387: Lease and release and mortgage, Goldsmid to Burdett and others 1834.

23 NLI, MS 13004(4): Letter from Mrs. Otway Cave to E.Taylour, 30 January 1848.

24 NA, CSORP OP: 1847 TY 27/1995.

25 NA, SOC 1827 2834/47.

26 NLI, MS 18,418 Xerox letters and petitions from tenants to Robert Otway Cave, originals are in the Leicester City Archives.

27 NA, CSORP OP: TY 1838 27/1362.

28 NA, SOC 1815 1721/42.

29 NA, CSORP OP:TY 1840 27/17527.

30 NA, SOC 1815 1721/42.

31 NA, CSORP OP:TY 1847 27/30219,TY 1848 27/282.

32 *TV*, 31 Jan 1844.

33 *TV*, 13 July 1844.

34 Vaughan, *Landlord and tenants*, p. 15.

35 John Coolahan, 'The daring first decade of the Board of National Education 1831–41', in *The Irish Journal of Education*, xvii, no.1 & 2, (1983) p. 38.

36 NA, ED.9 /27512: National Board of Education.

37 The Cooneyites or Dippers were associated with the Baptist movement.

38 Representative Church Body Library, Dublin, Church of Ireland parish of Templederry select vestrymen, 1870–1949.

39 NA,Tipperary ED 1/82 no. 26, National Board of Education.

40 Kevin Whelan, 'The Catholic church in County Tipperary 1700–1900' in William Nolan (ed.), *Tipperary: history and society* (Dublin, 1985), pp 215–55.

41 *First report of the commissioners of public instruction, Ireland with appendix to first report*, H.C. 1835 [45][46] xxxiii.i.829.

42 Ignatius Murphy, *The diocese of Killaloe 1800–1850* (Dublin, 1992), pp 342–47.

43 *NG*, 20 March 1841.

44 *TV*, 13 Aug 1845.

45 L.M. Fogarty, *Fr. Kenyon, a patriot priest of '48* (Dublin, 1920).

46 NLI, MS 13004(4)): Letter from Mrs. Otway Cave to Wm Stephens 10 Nov 1848.

47 Rev. John Clancy 'Some parish priests of Templederry' in *Molua*, 1949, pp 32–42, p. 42.

48 Clancy 'Some parish priests of Templederry' pp 32–42, p. 42.

49 NLI, MS 13004(4): Letter from Fr. John Kenyon to Edwin Taylor 29 May 1847.

50 Catholic parish register Templederry 27 Sept 1860.

51 NLI, MS 12139: Ledger 1778–9.

52 James Kelly, 'Select documents XLIII: a secret return of Volunteers of Ireland in 1784' in *Irish Historical Studies*, xxvi, no. 103 (1989), pp 268–92.

53 Sir Richard Musgrave, *Memoirs of the different rebellions in Ireland* ... 4th ed. Steven W. Myers and Ryan Taylor (Indiana, 1995), pp 670–1, 848.

54 Musgrave, *Memoirs*, p. 848.

55 M.R. Beams, 'Rural conflict in pre-famine Ireland', in *Past and present*, no. 81, (1978), pp 75–91.

56 Maurice J. Bric, 'The Whiteboy movement in Tipperary, 1760–80' in Nolan (ed.), *Tipperary: history and society*, pp 169–84; James W. Hurst, 'Disturbed Tipperary, 1831–60, in *Éire-Ireland*, ix, (1974), pp 44–59;

57 NA, SOC 1815 1721/61, 1721/89.

58 NA, SOC 1815 1721/56.

59 NA, SOC 1815 1721/39.

60 NA, SOC 1825 2834/59.

61 NA, CSORP OP: NA, TY 1848 27/446, 27/573, 27/626, 27/652, 27/7310, 27/875.

62 *TV*, 19 June 1844.

63 *TV*, 19 June 1844.

64 *TV*, 20 Oct 1847.

65 Denis Gwynn, 'The rising of 1848' in *Studies*, xxxvii, no. 145, 1948, p. 14.

66 NA, ED1/82 No. 26 Application for grants for Templederry and Latteragh national schools.

67 *TV*, 11 Dec 1844.

68 *TV*, 8 Nov 1845

69 Irish Folklore Commission, Schools Collection, Irish Folklore Commission, primary schools' collection, Curreeny National School, Templederry, County Tipperary, p. 30.

70 Irish Folklore Commission, Schools Collection, Irish Folklore Commission, primary schools' collection, Templederry National School, Templederry, County Tipperary, p. 94

71 NA, RCP, R 3/1/1754.

72 NA, RCP, R 3/1/1754.

73 NA, RCP, R 3/1/2162.

74 NA, RCP, R 3/1/1569.

75 NA, RCP, R 3/1/2307.

76 NA, RCP, R 3/1/2496.

CONCLUSION

1 Peter Somerville-Large, *The Irish county house: a social history* (London, 1995), p. 210; Michael Hewson, 'Eighteenth-century directions to servants in County Tipperary ' in Etienne Rynne (ed.), *North Munster studies, essays in commemoration of Monsignor Michael Moloney* (Limerick, 1967), pp 332–4.

2 Bruce Elliott, *Irish migrants in the Canadas: a new approach* (Belfast, 1988), p. xxi.

3 *Census of Ireland for the year 1851, showing the area, population and number of houses enumerated by townlands and electoral division,* (*Tipperary, North Riding*), pp 291–3, H.C. 1852–53 [1549], xci 383–723.

4 Cormac Ó Gráda, *The great Irish famine* (Dublin, 1989), p. 20.

5 Irish Folklore Commission, primary schools collection, Curreeny national school, Templederry, County Tipperary, reel number 537, p. 38.

6 Irish Folklore Commission, primary schools collection, Templederry national school, Templederry, County Tipperary, reel number 537, p. 100.